About the Author

LOUISE LAMBERT-LAGACÉ, mother of three daughters, sees patients in a private clinic and is a nutrition consultant. She received a B.Sc. (nutrition), is a member of the Canadian Dietetic Association, current Board member of the Society for Nutrition Education, and Chairperson of the Science and Technology Advisory Committee, Canadian Broadcasting Corporation, French network.

FEEDING YOUR CHILD

Louise Lambert-Lagacé

EXLEY

First Published in Great Britain in 1984 by Exley Publications Ltd,
16 Chalk Hill, Watford, Herts WD1 4BN
© 1982 by Louise Lambert-Lagacé
© this British edition 1984 by Louise Lambert-Lagacé

Cover Photo by courtesy of Tony Stone Associates

British Library Cataloguing in Publication Data

Lambert-Lagacé, Louise
    Feeding your child.
    1. Children – Nutrition   2. Cookery
    3. Infants – Nutrition
    I. Title   II. Comment nourir son enfant.
    English
    613.2'088054   RJ206

    ISBN 1-85015-005-2

Printed and bound in Great Britain by Hazell Watson and Viney Limited,
member of the BPCC Group, Aylesbury, Bucks.

Contents

Foreword

NUTRITION IS IMPORTANT at any age but particularly so during periods of rapid growth, during pregnancy, nursing, and infancy. Malnutrition during infancy not only jeopardizes development and health at that age, but may prevent the attainment of full physical and intellectual potential. Conversely, overnutrition at an early age may lead to the multiplication of fat cells, which may make lifelong obesity more likely. This overnutrition, incidentally, is often the result of early and excessively generous introduction of solid food particularly in children who are artificially fed. (Breast-feeding, besides its psychological advantages to the mother and the child, provides the baby with nutrients in optimal proportion.)

Specifically, excessive salt intake in infancy has been linked to hypertension in middle age. Excessive sugar intake throughout life has been linked to an increase in the likelihood of diabetes in genetically susceptible persons. All in all, nutrition in infancy and childhood is or should be a subject of abiding interest to professionals and parents.

Louise Lagacé brings to this subject the experience of a well-trained nutritionist and nutrition educator. Known in the field for the clarity of her style, for the care with which she researches the subject and for the sprightliness and charm with which she expresses it, she is particularly well qualified to give the practical advice that is needed. The French edition of her book has been very successful; I trust that this second English edition, fully revised and updated will be equally popular.

Jean Mayer, Ph.D., D.Sc., A.M. (hon.), S.D. (hon), M.D. (hon.)

Acknowledgements

L ISON CHAUVIN-DÉSOURDY, dietitian, actively participated in the bibliographical research, the review of baby foods, the calculation of the nutritive value of the menus, and the testing of new recipes. For more than eighteen months her enthusiasm and conscientiousness were extremely valuable.

Dr René Benoit, the paediatrician of my three daughters since their birth, encouraged me greatly by carefully reviewing the manuscript. His suggestions enabled me to adapt the theoretical to the practical.

Dr Jacques Letarte, Associate Professor in the Faculty of Medicine at the Université de Montréal, Paediatrician and Chief of Endocrinology and Metabolism at Sainte-Justine's Hospital, also scrupulously reread the text. His comments lend additional credibility to the book, for which I am indeed grateful.

Dr Jean Mayer, president of Tufts University in Boston, by writing the Foreword, gave the book such a precious seal of approval! I wish to thank him most sincerely.

Cynthia Dougherty, dietitian, doctoral student and mother of a one-year-old, worked scrupulously on the manuscript to incorporate the most recent information for the 1982 edition.

To all these valuable collaborators from start to finish, thank you again.

Introduction

AFTER FIVE YEARS on the Canadian market and initial sales of 150,000 copies, *Feeding Your Child* has been revised to incorporate the most recent scientific data.

Since the publication of the first edition in 1974, hundreds of parents have asked me questions about various aspects of nutrition for children. These questions subsequently helped me to pinpoint parental concerns and to guage better the type of information required. They also contributed significantly to determining the direction this second edition should take.

In addition, during the same period, considerable research was conducted to better define the nutritional needs of young children and to evaluate the effects of feeding during the first years of life on the future health of an individual. Not all these questions have been answered completely, but several professional bodies and government departments have developed guidelines on the subject.

This second edition reflects the established consensus on child feeding from conception to eighteen months of age.

It remains a practical and easy guide for planning delicious and nutritious meals, introducing solid foods, and for preparing baby foods at home.

I sincerely hope that the book, in its revised and rejuvenated form, will help all parents who are concerned about feeding their children well.

L.L.L.

CHAPTER ONE

The Importance of Feeding Your Child Well

FIFTY YEARS AGO, a child's food was closely scrutinized to ensure normal growth and protect the child from malnutrition. Today, we aim for long-term healthful effects through good nutritious foods provided during the first few years of life. Thus we hope to prevent and even eliminate the two greatest enemies to health: obesity and cardiovascular diseases.

What are the important considerations concerning feeding and the health of a child during the first months of life?

Firstly one should not give a child regular cow's milk before six months of age, and should not introduce solid foods until the baby has reached four months of age. This can greatly reduce the problems of anaemia and dehydration.

Can good nutrition during the first year of life have long-term health benefits for an individual?

Teaching the child to choose wholesome foods and to eat reasonable portions is the first step in the right direction. By encouraging good food habits, for example, the risk of obesity is reduced, although this is not absolutely guaranteed. Good food habits should be continued for many years for the child to benefit as much as possible.

Does a fat baby necessarily become an obese adult?

Currently, there are several sides to this question. In 80% of all cases, a fat baby at birth is not fat at one year, and will not necessarily be fat as an adult. However, a baby that gains weight too rapidly during the first year of life has a greater chance of becoming obese over the long term than a fat baby with a normal growth curve in relation to his birth weight.

We now know that there are several periods of intense fat-cell multiplication during childhood and adolescence, and that this multiplication is greatest during the first twelve months. If an eight-month-old baby eats much more than he needs, he stimulates the multiplication of fat cells. Although not completely reversible, this occurrence can be partially corrected during the following years when feeding is readjusted to the needs of the child. Irreversible obesity at one year is a myth, whereas normal weight at the end of adolescence is a quasi-prediction of long-term normal weight.

How can you prevent obesity?

A fat baby should not be deprived of food or given skimmed milk before six months but it is recommended that his weight curve be followed closely and the rate of weight gain be watched, especially in families with obesity problems.

Can we prevent cardiovascular problems at a young age?

Cholesterol deposits in tissues start to form in the first year of life, but are reversible up to age twenty. By systematically avoiding certain foods, the formation of irreversible plaques can be delayed and perhaps serious cardiovascular problems could even be avoided. Care is especially necessary in families with a history of cardiovascular disease.

What foods should you avoid giving to young children with high cholesterol levels?

Egg yolk, offal (liver, kidneys, heart), processed meats (pâtés, sausages, salami), cream, butter, coconut, and chocolate should be eliminated from the menu. A relatively strict diet should be adhered to for hyper-cholesterolemic children. In order to balance the diets of such children, their families should consult specialists in the field, and dietitians.

Can cardiovascular diseases be prevented among children from healthy families by applying the same restrictions?

Although the moderate consumption of foods rich in saturated fats (meats, processed meats, butter, cheese) and cholesterol, is beneficial, a menu containing less meat, more fish, poultry, fruit, vegetables and whole-grain cereals, as well as low-fat dairy products, ensures the growth of the child and can limit cardiovascular problems over the long term.

Can tooth decay, a widespread problem among our children, be remedied?

This problem can be greatly reduced during childhood and effective long-term prevention can be practised:

- avoid, at all costs, covering the dummy with honey or syrup to help the baby sleep.
- give the child a fluoride supplement from the first year of life if municipal water is not fluoridated
- limit the consumption of concentrated sweets by the child, particularly at snack time
- teach the child, at an early age, to brush his or her teeth regularly.

The beneficial effects of sound nutrition don't stop at disease prevention and reduction of tooth decay. One by one we will be featuring in this book the beneficial effects of breast-feeding, the gradual introduction of solids, and healthy menus for your tiny tots.

CHAPTER TWO

Good Eating Habits
Begin in the Cradle

IMPLANTED IN one's memory, eating habits are formed year after year from our taste experiences. Far from being static, they evolve during one's lifetime, always reflecting immediate family influences and the cultural environment. During childhood, these eating habits crystallise around familiar foods and traditional mealtime rituals.

A child who gulps down fried foods and sweets 'between commercials' on TV, or who eats few fruits and vegetables and consistently quenches his thirst with soft drinks or coloured fruit-flavoured beverages, does not retain the same sensory information as the child initiated at a very young age to 'healthy' foods.

Developing a taste for food which has undergone a minimum of processing, and which is only slightly sweetened or salted, occurs gradually and painlessly in an environment where varied and healthy eating habits are practised. On the other hand, it is much harder for an adult to reverse previously acquired poor eating habits.

The general attitude regarding food and the various 'non-verbal' messages transmitted daily to a child have as much to do with the forming of eating habits as the food itself.

Healthy Foods, Fun Foods

Eating is essentially enjoyable and is as much a pleasure as it is a human need. There are many ways to associate pleasure with healthy foods and, when healthy food habits are repeatedly practised by the family, the child is encouraged to develop those habits. Therefore:

- By regularly serving green, yellow, and white vegetables, cooked or raw, which can be munched on between meals by everyone, a child will rapidly accept them regardless of the normal reticence typical to the pre-school years.
- Parents' obvious anticipation and expressed pleasure with spring's first greens, summer's new peas, potatoes and salads, autumn's runner beans and winter's root crops, and enthusiasm for a variety of vegetables, will help their children to develop a positive attitude towards these foods and encourage them to try other new food experiences.
- Regular purchases of all kinds of fish and shellfish help familiarize a child with the real taste of seafood and lead him to culinary experiences that go beyond frozen fish fingers or breaded fish cakes.
- Fresh fruit for dessert is readily accepted by a child who has not become accustomed to a regular diet of pies or cakes; to him, fruit is a reflection of the seasons and will never be a 'poor dessert substitute for weight-loss diets.'
- Frequent consumption of vegetarian dishes based on pulses will subtly dispel the steak myth, while the time is ripe.

To enjoy sound and tasty foods is the best and most positive way to introduce a healthy diet to a child; this obviously implies that parents eat well themselves. But do not leave out the odd treat. Once or twice will do no harm.

Food – A Source of Physical and Emotional Satisfaction

Fed when hungry, the infant is physically satisfied; cuddled and comforted in the arms of his mother, while being breast-fed, he is also emotionally satisfied. To any infant, physical and emotional satisfaction is associated with meals and with maternal warmth. Both satisfy two distinct needs – hunger, and the need for affection. This interaction could confuse the child if one is not careful.

The child who is fed whenever he cries, or is overfed to make him sleep longer, cannot, after a few weeks, differentiate between the need to eat and other discomforts. Food becomes the solution to all problems: the need for attention, the need for affection, and the need for diversion.

For several years, Dr Hilde Bruch, a psychiatrist, has attempted to shed some light on specific eating behaviours (bulimia or uncontrolled eating, obesity, anorexia), and has found that these problems are directly linked to early childhood experiences. When this behaviour becomes evident, food does not meet nutritional needs but instead symbolizes almost exclusively the following needs in order of importance or frequency:

- an insatiable desire for inaccessible love
- an expression of rage or hatred
- an ascetic refusal
- a substitute for sexual gratification
- a defence against maturity and responsibilities
- a false sensation of power.

Based upon information collected from many case studies, Dr Bruch stresses that the hunger mechanism requires proper training to develop normally – we are not necessarily born with large or small appetites:

- we learn to be hungry when it is time
- we learn to know when to stop
- we can easily unlearn early in life.

An infant who is forced to finish his bottle or clean his plate is not learning how to control his appetite, while a baby who nurses at the breast for more than thirty minutes is often nursing too long. This means that from the very first weeks a mother can teach a child to recognize various bodily needs and to satisfy them appropriately.

It Takes Two to Recognize Satiety

Mother and child both have a role to play in the normal development of the baby's hunger mechanism. Although not a totally dependent human being, a newborn child is capable of expressing his needs and desires within the first few hours of life:

- he can cry, cough, swallow, vomit
- he can smell and hear
- he can distinguish between pain and touch
- he can turn his head in the direction his cheek is touched
- he can twist and kick his feet.

To help the child in his role, the mother must respond to his actions and react correctly to his messages, thereby allowing him to get to know himself better.

A mother who feeds a child to appease all crying, and to console or comfort, is not interpreting her child's messages properly. But a mother who offers foods in reply to real cries of hunger, contributes to the development of a baby's hunger mechanism. The right reaction at the right moment is one of the key factors influencing the baby's eating behaviour.

Should a child refuse to drink the last ounce in his bottle, a mother should not insist he does, but rather respect the child as an individual. When he refuses to eat after having eaten a fair amount, he is saying that he has had enough. This sign of satiety should be respected.

If your baby refuses meat or some vegetable when you start introducing different solids into his diet, you would do better to let him have his own way, and give him the disputed item at another meal, accompanied by some other food of which he is very fond. His acceptance of new foods will only come about gradually, and will need your patience and understanding. To force him to swallow a given food shows a lack of respect for your child. After all, even adults have their little whims.

When there is a loss of appetite, do not force the child to eat because you feel that he must eat to be healthy. Appetites vary during the first years of life. A loss of appetite usually happens when the child's rate of growth has slowed down.

The mother who understands and reacts correctly to messages from her child enables him to participate actively in the feeding process.

Love on the Menu

Ecology plays a vital role in a house plant's development. However, water and light are not the only factors necessary in making it thrive. A plant apparently grows faster and blossoms more readily if spoken to and placed among 'good company.' Also, certain types of music supposedly stimulate its growth. In short, it is affected by a favourable environment.

For optimum growth and development, a child also has ecological needs which must be satisfied which go beyond the traditional nutritive needs; food alone is not enough. Other important elements, such as parental affection, should be added to the daily menu to create a healthy environment.

This socio-affective 'food-environment' association has been the subject of considerable research among children of Latin-American countries, research aimed at minimizing the effects of malnutrition. One of the studies involved weight gain and health status comparisons between one group of infants given supplementary foods during the first six months of life, and a control group of babies from the same Guatemalian village who did not receive supplementary food.

The 'supplemented infants,' who were from larger, poorer, and less educated families, gained less weight and were sick more often during the six-month period than were the non-supplemented infants. The extra food did not counteract the effects of their disadvantaged environment.

This somewhat extreme example shows the importance of the environment and of other factors, such as attention and affection, necessary for the proper total nourishment of a child.

Another study showed a positive relationship between the nutritional state of young children and the verbal communication which existed between mother and child. The greater the exchange of sounds or language between mother and child, the better was the child's nutritional state.

You see, it is a question of a favourable environment.

Sharing Meals

Meals are pleasurable social moments for adults. Not only food is shared, but ideas and feelings as well. To a child, however small, taking part in the family meal becomes one of his first social activities. When he starts feeding himself, the meal becomes a privileged moment during which he has his own place at the table.

Eating with the family does not mean that a toddler must always have what others are eating. Rather, it implies social integration and active participation in a family activity.

The late Doctor Jean Trémolières stressed the important aspects of the family meal when he wrote: 'Finally, the very simple rites of the family table delineate those two images without which no civilization has hitherto existed, without which, psychoanalysis tells us, it is almost impossible for us to develop our own personal equilibrium: namely, the Mother and the Father. Food takes on a symbolic aspect, in which its intrinsic qualities are combined with the special qualities with which we endow it.'

Mealtime – A Time to Relax

Meals should occur in a pleasant atmosphere, and should not be a time for reprimands, quarrels, or violent arguments. A tension-filled atmosphere can curb a preschool child's often fragile appetite. If a child associates mealtime with battle-time, he will never experience the pleasurable aspects of mealtime, essential to forming good food habits.

A child should never be forced to accept certain foods; he could become a little tyrant should parents try to do so. A meal would therefore become a power struggle between the parents forcing the child to eat, and the child, time and time again, refusing certain foods.

Professor A.S. Neill, well-known author of *The Free Children of Summerhill,* describes in his book *Freedom, Not License* the following phenomenon: 'With a child, an eating problem embodies a certain element of protest. The child uses his food preferences at the table to proclaim: "I'm the boss here, so listen to me." '

Whims

Without eliminating whims completely, it is possible to circumvent them in order to maintain a balanced diet for the child. No food is completely irreplacable.

A wise mother can substitute one food with another of equal nutritive value without detriment to the child. A child who systematically refuses cooked vegetables will often crunch away quite happily at raw vegetables, and a child who refuses milk will perhaps accept yogurt, cheese, ice-cream, or a fruit-flavoured milk. In the same way that one learns to respect the newborn baby's appetite for his bottle and his first solid foods, so it is equally important to respect the likes and dislikes of the preschool child. This respect does not imply surrender or an acceptance of the child's whim – rather, it implies a fuller understanding on the part of parents who are determined to feed their child properly.

These whims allow a child to display his personality and individuality, and appear in the preschool child at a time when his appetite normally decreases. If parents react properly to such refusals and to momentary whims, and if war is not declared at each meal, a child will give in without realizing it. Being overly forceful about this or that food puts more negative emphasis on a particular type of food and can provoke such a reaction in the child that he will dislike the food for life. This is hardly conducive to the formation of good eating habits.

The more myths and taboos a child builds up about various foods, the more quickly will he close the door to a wide variety of foods, and this makes a sound and balanced diet difficult to attain in adulthood.

Actions Speak Louder than Words

Parents must also be aware of the logical consequences of their own actions. At the risk of sounding repetitious, proper eating habits are not acquired at a neighbour's or elsewhere, but by observing father and mother eating three times a day, 365 days a year.

A child who can appreciate the joy of eating a variety of foods from the start does not need to know the merits of vitamin C, iron, or other elements essential for growth. After all, do we wish to raise a child dietitian or simply a happy person enjoying tasty and healthy food?

The following anecdote illustrates the advantages of an approach that stressed healthy, good-tasting foods as opposed to a nutrition course adapted to the very young: 'I really liked eating spinach until my mother told me it was good for me.'

Without knowing it, the child will be conditioned to enjoy eating, and this remains the greatest hope of nutritionists at this time.

CHAPTER THREE

The Prenatal Diet

ALTHOUGH THIS CHAPTER cannot cover all aspects of prenatal nutrition, it nevertheless gives broad dietary guidelines which should be put into practice long before the birth of the child.

Unfortunately, the recipe for a bouncing, healthy baby is not simply two cups of love combined with two cups of hope, left to simmer over a nine-month period. Other elements greatly influence the final product, such as the mother's health before conception, and her diet during pregnancy. It must be remembered that life begins at conception and than an important legacy is begun before birth.

Diet Intervention

Even in our medically well-equipped industrialized society, the birth of a healthy child remains a feat. Many mothers succeed brilliantly; some, unfortunately, lose their babies during pregnancy or at birth; and others give birth to babies of below normal weight, who sometimes have physical and mental defects.

In the UK in 1982, 13,281 babies were born with some kind of birth defect. This was 210.9 per 10,000 births. In the same year 39,933 were born in England and Wales weighing less than 2.5 kg (5.5 lb), 1,442 of these were born weighing less than 1 kg (2.2 lb). There were 625,931 live births. The infant mortality rate for the UK was 12.6 per 1,000 live births.

In order to avoid many of these problems, and to really help expectant mothers, more and more diet interventions are being provided. The results of these programmes strikingly underline the tremendous importance of good nutrition during pregnancy. Here are a few examples of effective diet intervention:

- For more than thirty years, dietitians in Montreal have helped low-income pregnant women to plan adequate, well-balanced diets. In addition, they provide milk, eggs, and oranges without charge to the neediest of their clients. From 1963 to 1972, among one group of mothers, the number of low birth-weight babies (less than $5\frac{1}{2}$ lb.) was cut in half, and the number of deaths during the first weeks of life was reduced by two-thirds. The 'improved' prenatal diet was not the only responsible factor, but it certainly played an important role.
- In the United States, the Special Supplemental Food Program for Women, Infants, and Children (WIC) is aimed at providing supplemental foods to assist participants in obtaining an adequate diet. In the UK the physical welfare of all pregnant women is carefully watched. From the thirty-second week of pregnancy all women attend the ante-natal clinic at the hospital where their baby will be born. The development of the fetus will be monitored, scans will be taken if necessary and the mother's general health and weight gain will be carefully watched. In some hospitals there will be a dietician on hand to advise her on diet while she is pregnant. Vitamin and iron supplements will be provided, free of charge, if these are deemed necessary in her case. The Department of Health and Social Security runs a scheme offering free milk and vitamins for expectant mothers and children up to the age of five years in low income families. In addition free dental treatment and free medical prescriptions are available for all expectant and nursing mothers.
- At Harvard University, the number of low birth-weight babies born in 1977 in four regions of the State of Massachusetts was calculated, and it was discovered that there were nearly five times fewer small babies (less than $5\frac{1}{2}$ lb.) born to mothers whose diets had been adjusted during pregnancy, as compared to mothers whose diets had been left to chance.

A Question of Pounds

To our grandmothers, a pregnancy was almost a dream come true because they could eat to their hearts' content. They accepted the more or less permanent weight gain as part of being a mother, and were thoroughly convinced of the necessity of eating a great deal in order to produce a healthy baby. Doctors burdened by complications at delivery often pointed the finger at excessive weight gain, and that caused an abrupt about-face in prenatal eating habits.

Towards the end of the '50s, a pregnant woman's eating habits were cause for remorse which lasted nine months, as she feared both the scale and reprisal from her doctor; a weight gain of only 5 to 8 kg (15 to 18 lb.) was allowed. This was a period of tiny pregnant women, mini-babies, and a new series of complications.

In the UK ante-natal clinics recommend an overall weight gain of around 11 kg (24 lb.).

This wise and realistic recommendation was the result of much observation and many scientific surveys which demonstrated that a properly nourished pregnant woman gives birth to a normal-weight baby, with optimal chances for survival and normal physical and mental development. We also know that the weight of the baby at birth generally reflects a mother's diet and her weight gain during pregnancy, and that it can also determine the baby's future development and well being.

A below-normal weight gain during pregnancy is associated with the birth of a smaller baby. Thus, the World Health Organization feels that a baby weighing less than $5\frac{1}{2}$ pounds at birth has fewer chances for survival and for good health than a normal-weight baby delivered at term (3.3 to 3.5 kg or 7 to 8 lb.).

Well-Used Pounds

One might imagine, perhaps, that weight gained during pregnancy goes directly to the baby and that any excess stays on the mother's hips. In reality, it is more complex.

One-third of the weight gained during the nine months goes directly to the baby. The other two-thirds is used for 'auxiliary services,' the enlarged uterus providing the fetus with a made-to-measure lodging, the placenta becoming a mobile canteen, and the amniotic fluid, a water bed. The 33% increase in the mother's blood content, her tissues and breasts, ensures the baby's better feeding before and after birth. Only a few pounds remain as maternal reserves to facilitate the mother's recovery after delivery and to provide sufficient energy during breast-feeding. In round numbers, the weight gained during the nine months of pregnancy is distributed as follows:

fetus	7 lb.	(3.2 kg)
placenta	1.5 lb.	(0.7 kg)
amniotic fluid	2 lb.	(0.9 kg)
uterus	2 lb.	(0.9 kg)
breasts	1 lb.	(0.4 kg)
blood volume	3 lb.	(1.4 kg)
tissue fluids	3 lb.	(1.4 kg)
fat deposits	6 lb.	(2.7 kg)
TOTAL	25.5 lb.	(11.6 kg)

A Regular Weight Gain

A gradual weight gain during the nine months of pregnancy corresponds more favourably to the fetus's and the mother's needs than a large but irregular gain. The total weight gained is less important than the rate of gain, because the latter has to follow a curve which reflects both the baby's and the mother's needs during the entire pregnancy.

Even if the fetus's growth is slow during the first three months, the energy level required from the internal reorganization of the mother's body, previously referred to as 'auxiliary services,' cannot be underestimated. A 1 to 2 kg (2 to 4 lb) weight gain is recommended during the first trimester.

During the next six months, a gain of about 0.4 kg (1 lb)

per week fulfils the fetus's growth requirements. This means a weight gain of about 11 to 13 kg (24 to 30 lb.) for the whole pregnancy.

Weight-Loss Diets Strictly Contra-Indicated

Pregnancy is not the time to try to lose weight. An overweight or obese mother should not try to lose weight at this crucial time, for a menu containing fewer than 1,800 calories would deprive her of vital nutritive elements and would deprive the fetus as well. A pregnant woman who draws on her body fat for energy to compensate for the lack of food, endangers the physical and mental development of her child. It is better to lose weight *before or after* pregnancy if the good of the child and mother is to be kept in mind.

Nutrition Adapted for Two

Medically speaking, an appropriate diet during pregnancy reduces the risks during delivery, permits the growth of a healthy baby, produces good maternal reserves, and prepares the mother for breast-feeding.

These arguments strongly favour a proper diet and should encourage mothers-to-be to eat better. Many are aware of this but unfortunately, not everyone. A recent survey of more than 400 pregnant women showed that nearly two-thirds of these women ate more fruit, vegetables, and milk products, and consumed fewer sweets and carbonated beverages during pregnancy. In spite of these positive elements, however, consumption of liver or other offal was definitely insufficient while the consumption of bread and cereal and milk products was slightly insufficient. Other surveys reveal the same findings.

An adequate prenatal diet does not involve that great a change when good eating habits are present from the start. The main changes to the daily menu are practically unnoticeable at the beginning and do not disrupt the family's menu. The portions gradually increase in a pregnant woman's menu, but all additions are derived from the basic food groups and are easily found and prepared.

Regarding calories, a supplement of 100-150 calories per day for the first three months is recommended, and 300-350 calories per day during the second and third trimesters. During the first three months, 100-150 calories can be built up easily by adding one of the following to the daily menu:

III-1: *100-150 Calories More per Day*

- 6-8 oz. (180-250ml) of semi-skimmed milk
  or
- 1-1½ oz. (30-45 gm) of hard cheese (Edam, Mozzarella, etc.)
  or
- 1 scrambled egg
  or
- 1-2 slices of whole-wheat bread with butter or margarine
  or
- 4-6 oz. (120-180 gm) of fruit yogurt

During the second and third trimesters, the 300-350 extra calories are integrated gradually by supplementing the menu with the required dairy products and other important foods.

In terms of protein, a gradual increase in the intake of protein-rich foods is recommended from the start of the pregnancy in order to attain about 80 grams of protein at the beginning of the fourth month of pregnancy. One can obtain 80 grams of protein by eating daily:

III-2: *80 Grams of Protein per Day*

- 4-4½ oz. (120-135 gm) of meat,
  poultry or seafood .... 30 grams
- 1 egg .... 7 grams
- 1 litre (or 2 pints) of milk or its
  equivalent in dairy products* .... 32-35 grams
- 3 to 4 portions of whole-grain cereal
  products (e.g. 1 bowl of cereal, 1 slice
  of bread) .... 9-12 grams

                                        78-84 grams/day

The 'vegetarian' pregnant woman, who does not eat meat, poultry, or fish, but who does take milk products and eggs, will consume 80 grams of protein by eating daily:

III-3: *80 Grams of Protein per Day in a Vegetarian Menu*

- 1 cup of cooked pulses (beans, peas lentils) .... 12 grams
- 6 to 7 portions of whole-grain cereal products (1 slice of bread, 1 bowl of cereal) .... 12 grams
- 3 tablespoons of nuts or seeds .... 9 grams
- 1 litre of milk or its equivalent in dairy products* .... 32-35 grams
- 1 egg .... 7 grams

78-84 grams/day

*I cup (250 ml) of milk = 8 oz. (240 gm) of yogurt = 1½ oz. (45 gm) of cheese

In terms of calcium intake, it is recommended that 400-500 mg per day be added to the 700-800 mg already required in the normal woman's daily diet. The prenatal diet would thus include 1,200 mg in total, which would be obtained by eating the following each day:

III-4: *1,200 Mg of Calcium per Day*

- 1 litre (2 pints) of milk .... 1,189 mg/day
  or
- 1½ oz. (45 gm) of hard cheese (Edam, Mozzarella) .... 300 mg/day
- 8 oz. (240 gm) of yogurt (plain or fruit) .... 400 mg/day
- 1 8-oz. (250 ml) glass of milk .... 300 mg/day
- 4 oz. (125 ml) of milk with cereal .... 150 mg/day

1,150 mg/day

Besides dairy products, a few foods provide 150 to 200 mg

of calcium per serving, such as canned salmon, sardines and mackerel, providing they are eaten complete with bones.

It is recommended in the UK that iron consumption be increased by 3 mg, which brings the total necessary for a pregnant woman to 15 mg per day. Since little iron is eliminated once absorbed, the weekly consumption of iron-rich foods that are easily absorbed by the body (offal, ie., liver, kidney, heart and brains) allows the accumulation of a reserve of this precious nutrient for other days of the week.

III-5: *20 Mg of Iron per Day*

• 4 oz. (120 gm) of beef	4-7.5 mg
• 5 portions of whole-grain cereal products	10 mg
• 5 portions of fruit and vegetables	2.5 mg
	16.5-20 mg/day

The vegetarian pregnant woman obtains her daily iron needs by eating:

III-6: *Daily Iron in a Vegetarian Menu*

• 1 cup (250 ml) of cooked pulses	5 mg
• 6 to 7 portions of whole-grain cereal products	12-14 mg
• 5 portions of fruit and vegetables	2.5 mg
	19.5-21.5 mg/day

While iron found in vegetable-type foods is harder to absorb, the additional quantities contained in a vegetarian diet help compensate for this fact. Eaten with vitamin C-rich fruits and vegetables, iron is absorbed five times better than it would be otherwise.

A pregnant woman requires additional amounts of vitamins and minerals. However, if she regularly eats the above-listed foods, rich in calcium, protein, and iron in appropriate quantities, she also absorbs *all the other nutritive elements in adequate amounts*. Finally, and they are always the same, are the foods which supply the growing fetus its most essential needs:

- a litre (2 pints) of milk or its equivalent in dairy products contributes to both protein and calcium needs
- five servings of whole-grain cereal products (6 to 7 in a vegetarian diet) contribute to both protein and iron needs
- a cup of pulses or 4 to $4\frac{1}{2}$ oz. (120-135 gm) of meat contribute to both protein and iron needs
- five servings of fruit or vegetables contribute to both iron and vitamin needs

The servings suggested for each food group represent the *minimum* quantities which will satisfy the nutritive needs of a woman well-nourished prior to pregnancy. Quantities recommended in other recent publications I have seen represent maximum servings; these no doubt enable women who are malnourished at the beginning of pregnancy to overcome nutritional deficiencies.

The following typical menu provides a method of co-ordinating all these important foods during the day:

III-7: *Typical Menu for a Pregnant Woman*

With Meat	Vegetarian
1 citrus fruit or juice (125 ml)	1 citrus fruit or juice (125 ml)
whole-grain cereal	whole-grain cereal
4 oz. (125 ml) of milk	4 oz. (125 ml) of milk
1 whole-meal bap	2 whole-meal baps
1 6-oz. (180 ml) glass of milk	1 6-oz. (180 ml) glass of milk
1 egg	1 egg
$1\frac{1}{2}$ oz. (45 gm) cheese	$1\frac{1}{2}$ oz. (45 gm) cheese
raw or cooked vegetables	raw or cooked vegetables
whole-meal bread	whole-meal bread
1 fruit	1 fruit

6 oz. (180 gm) of yogurt *or*	6 oz. (180 gm) of yogurt *or*
1 6-oz. (180 ml) glass of milk	1 6-oz. (180 ml) glass of milk
soup or juice	soup or juice
4 to 4½ oz. (120-135 gm) of	serving of pulses (one
meat, poultry, or fish (offal	cup (250 ml) approximately)
once a week)	cooked or raw vegetables
cooked or raw vegetables	2 slices of whole-wheat bread
whole-wheat bread	1 fruit
1 fruit	1 8-oz. (250 ml) glass of milk
1 8-oz. (250 ml) glass of milk	

These typical menus reflect the *minimum* quantities of the four important food groups. The menus represent the needs of a sedentary woman weighing between 110 and 120 lb. (50-55 kg) at the time of conception. A more active or taller and stronger woman should increase the quantities in order to better satisfy her higher caloric requirements.

These foods can vary infinitely within each main category and be changed around throughout the day. In fact, the key to success lies in regular ingestion of calcium, iron, protein, and vitamin-rich foods, that is, foods which contribute towards making a healthy baby and maintaining maternal reserves.

Nausea and Heartburn

The fact that the digestion process is slowed down, hormone production is increased, and maternal reorganization favours the fetus's environment, means that the internal well-being of the pregnant woman can be upset. Nausea and heartburn are problems which affect a good number of mothers-to-be.

Miraculous and permanent solutions are rare. There exist, however, certain procedures to neutralize temporarily nausea and heartburn:

- eat a few water biscuits or crackers before getting up in the morning
- get up slowly in order to avoid sudden movements which could upset the stomach

- drinking should be avoided at mealtime: drink between meals only, that is thirty minutes after eating solids
- eat five or six small meals per day instead of three big ones and don't go more than two and-a-half to three hours without eating a sustaining snack
- avoid fried food, coffee and alcohol.

In most cases, these problems disappear before starting the second half of the pregnancy.

Are Supplements Needed?

Although a pregnant woman does not require in principle vitamin or mineral supplements, many are generally pre-scribed.

In the UK it is recommended by most doctors that pregnant women consume a supplement of iron and folic acid to compensate for possible poor eating habits.

In the aforementioned study on the dietary habits of pregnant women, the generalized prescription of large iron and vitamin C supplements is deplored. However, it is recognized that a certain number of women with deficient diets should be given supplements. Vitamin D and calcium supplements are particularly important when consumption of milk and dairy products is low.

Ideally, a medical team should be able to evaluate a pregnant woman's prenatal diet before prescribing a supplement; in practice, the attending physician has the last word.

Salt – Allowed or Banned?

Salt, the long-time enemy of the pregnant woman, is more often thought of as being something to eliminate rather than being a nutritious addition to a menu. A number of studies show, however, that the pregnant woman loses great quantities of salt or sodium and that her needs are slightly increased during pregnancy.

A large decrease in salt consumption brings about a

defence mechanism which causes tissues to retain water, an opposite effect to what was anticipated.

Alcohol – A Risky Luxury

Alcohol should not be drunk during pregnancy, since it can cause irreparable harm to the fetus. According to experts, during the first months of pregnancy consumption of 2 to 4 oz. (60 to 120 cc) of alcohol such as gin or whisky, can affect growth and cause physical and mental deficiencies in one out of ten fetuses. When the amount is increased beyond four ounces a day, the risks to the fetus increase proportionately and dangerously.

If we take into account the serious consequences and the difficulty in measuring the daily dose which would not present any risks, it seems foolish, at the present time, to recommend even moderate daily consumption.

Saccharin

Recently saccharin has attracted publicity on both sides of the Atlantic. It is thought possible, but not yet proved, that it is a cancer causing agent because animals fed large amounts of it have developed cancer. In the UK saccharin is still permitted as an additive, especially in soft drinks such as fruit squashes and diet drinks. However, under the Food and Drugs Act manufacturers are bound not only to control strictly the amount added but to state on the packaging that saccharin is in the food or drink. It is wise to avoid saccharin during pregnancy so check labels carefully before you buy packets, bottles and cans.

Aspartame

Aspartame (Nutra Sweet-Searle, Equal), a protein-based substance about 180 times as sweet as sugar, is available in the UK, under the brand name Canderel, to sweeten drinks, puddings, fillings and whipped toppings.

Long-term studies of the effects of Aspartame in people are not yet available: it would seem wise for pregnant and nursing women to remain prudent in their use of this sweetener, in any form.

Other Disputed Habits

From a study that included more than 190 pregnant women, Belgian researchers recently concluded that the consumption of large amounts of coffee (more than 8 cups per day) was associated with a higher rate of miscarriages and premature births. It is, therefore, recommended that coffee and caffeine-rich foods (Coca-Cola, tea, cocoa) should be avoided or at least taken in moderate quantities.

Decaffeinated coffee has also been reported to induce post-natal behaviour abnormalities in the offspring of rats. Certainly further investigation is warranted in humans but it seems wise to recommend that decaffeinated coffee be at least taken in moderation during pregnancy.

When more than twenty cigarettes are smoked daily, a baby's birth weight is lower than that of a baby of a non-smoking mother.

Prudence is the Password

The above precautions merely stress the fragility and vulnerability of the fetus with regard to maternal extravagances.

The placenta, the fetus's 'mobile canteen,' does not have a system which will remove suspicious substances; its membrane is as vulnerable to toxic substances as to essential elements. Properly supplied, it provides an excellent diet. Poorly supplied, the fetus's diet is impoverished, and the development of the child is affected.

A well-informed mother is worth her weight in gold. To obtain additional information on nutrition during pregnancy, contact your health visitor who will be happy to recommend helpful reading and to give you advice.

CHAPTER FOUR

A Super Baby Food

HUMAN MILK is without a doubt the best baby food, marvellously suited to the needs of a newborn child. Unique since the beginning of time, it is recommended for all babies. Unfortunately, a few generations of parents have erased the tradition, the custom, and its purpose.

For the past ten years, numerous studies on human milk and the milks of other mammals have been conducted throughout the world, helping us rediscover this truly amazing food we temporarily neglected.

A Ready-Made Food for the Species

It is absolutely fascinating to compare the principle ingredients that make up the milk of various mammals, enabling us to fully appreciate how nicely nature makes things.

The protein content in different milks varies according to the normal growth rate of each species. The more protein in the milk, the faster the species grows. The horse, for example, drinks 2% protein milk, and doubles its birth weight in sixty days, while the rabbit, fed milk six times as rich in protein (10% to 13%), doubles its weight in six days! Cow's milk, which contains 3.4% protein, enables the calf to double its weight in fifty days, while human milk, which contains 1% protein, enables a baby to double its weight in more than 100 days, that is, during the fourth or fifth month.

The amount of protein and minerals contained in milk influences the number of feedings necessary during a twenty-four-hour period. The more concentrated the milk, the longer the interval between feedings: rabbit's milk, which is very concentrated, entails one feeding per day, while human milk, being less concentrated, necessitates several feedings per day. Mice, which produce one of the most dilute milks, spend 80% of their day and night feeding their young!

The fat content of the various milks is related to the size of the animal and to the environmental temperature of the natural habitat of the animal concerned. The bigger the animal and the colder its environment, the higher the fat content of the milk. Thus elephant's milk contains 20% fat, seal's milk 43%, and that of the blue whale 50% fat.

The 'sugar' content of the milk varies according to the rate of brain development after birth. Accordingly human milk contains more sugar or lactose than the milk of any other mammal.

Nature Thinks of Everything

The kangaroo, which carries two young of different ages at the same time in its pouch, produces two kinds of milk: the younger animal drinks a concentrated milk, and when the older one nurses, it drinks from another nipple and receives a diluted milk more suitable to his needs.

The hokkaido monkey gives birth in the spring and nurses its young all summer. In the autumn, the mother lets the baby forage for himself, and replenishes herself. When snow appears and food is scarce, the young monkey resumes his intake of mother's milk – a seasonal pause.

Advantages for the Baby

Having been comfortably lodged in his mother's womb where he was kept warm and fed until delivery, life is not as easy for an infant after birth. He has to take charge of several functions himself: breathing, maintaining a proper body temperature, feeding himself and then digesting the food, fighting off infections, and so on. These first months of transition between his life as a fetus and his life 'outside' call for a proper diet given in an atmosphere of love and warmth.

Human milk fulfils the baby's needs completely. It supplies a baby's nutritive needs, provides incomparable immunological protection, and transmits numerous messages of love and affection.

A. A Marvellously Adapted Food

If human milk is broken down into its main nutritive components and is compared to other milks, it becomes immediately apparent how superior human milk is for children:

- The proteins contained in human milk are much easier to digest than proteins contained in cow's milk or in milk formulas. Once in the stomach, they coagulate into easily-digested tiny particles that are well utilized by the baby, unlike the harder and bigger particles found in cow's milk. Expressly intended for humans and subsequently present in the proper proportion, these proteins are without a doubt better suited to the needs of the newborn.
- The fatty substances in human milk represent not only an important source of calories and satiety value to the baby, but greatly contribute to brain development. Protein usually has been associated with this development, but today fatty acids are recognized as being equally important; 60% of the solid matter found in the brain is composed of these transformed fatty substances. Furthermore, during the first months following birth, 20% of the brain cells keeps on dividing (or multiplying). Human milk, which contains seven or eight times more essential fatty acids than whole cow's milk, provides an essential contribution.

  It should be noted that human milk does not supply these fatty elements continuously. Less abundant at the beginning of the feeding, they become more concentrated in the last few minutes of feeding at the breast. This unique phenomenon seems to favour appetite control in the breast-fed baby.

- Lactose, the type of sugar which is naturally present in all milk, is more abundant in human milk than in the milk of any other mammal, and for a very good reason. Once it has been partially transformed into galactose, lactose participates in the development of the nervous system and the growth of the brain, and it also favours calcium absorption.

- Iron contained in human milk was previously thought to be insufficient and present only in negligible quantities. We now know that it is very well absorbed by an infant due to the presence of large amounts of lactose and vitamin C, and because of the small amount of phosphorous and protein found in human milk. Furthermore, it has been found that babies who have been breast-fed rarely suffer from anaemia compared to babies fed cow's milk or simulated breast-milk formulas. These last observations confirm the effectiveness of iron in human milk. The amount of iron in human milk, furthermore, is sufficient for a full-term baby, of normal weight, until the age of six months or until solids are introduced.

- Regarding other mineral elements, human milk contains three times less calcium and six times less phosphorous than cow's milk. Too much phosphorous and calcium will tax the infant's renal system. Found in sufficient quantity in mother's milk, these minerals are important to the development and growth of bones and teeth.

- Zinc is present in large quantities in the colostrum-milk secreted during the first days following childbirth. Even if its concentration is reduced thereafter, the baby is better able to utilize the zinc present in human milk than that added to formulas. In fact, at the present time, it still has not been determined exactly how much zinc should be added to commercial formulas in order to achieve the same physiological effectiveness as the zinc in human milk.

- Human milk contains three times less sodium and potassium than cow's milk which makes it better suited to the baby's needs and his still underdeveloped renal system. Milk formulas adapted for babies contain equivalent quantities to those found in human milk.

- Vitamin D is only present in small quantities, but is found in a particularly active form and cannot be compared to that of cow's milk. It seems sufficiently available to the baby to protect him from rickets, although there are a few exceptions that we will mention in this chapter.
- The vitamin C contained in human milk varies slightly depending on the mother's diet but it is also manufactured internally by the mammary glands. It supplies a baby's needs entirely.
- Vitamin A and the B-complex vitamins are found in sufficient amounts in human milk as well as in cow's milk and formulas.

Human milk has a nutritive quality which never ceases to amaze. A breast-fed baby does not require additional consumption of water, as his water reserves are adequate after drinking human milk. This is even true for hot and humid days. Milk from a mother who has delivered a premature baby contains more proteins than that of a mother whose baby was born at term, thus satisfying the greater protein needs of a premature baby. This milk, however, does not contain sufficient quantities of all the nutrients needed to satisfy the immense requirements of a very small premature baby, but is nevertheless better suited to the needs of a premature infant than any other milk formula.

B. Happy Effects

The numerous nutritive benefits of human milk are reflected by the general state of health of the infant. Any health professional knows this.

A study has been carried out to verify certain effects of breast-feeding on the baby's well-being. A small amount of blood was taken from 556 infants; some were breast-fed, some bottle-fed. It was found that at six months and at one year the breast-fed babies' blood contained greater quantities of folic acid and vitamins A, E, and C than that of the other babies. Another study made of babies under six months of age revealed that the breast-fed babies had a better weight for their age and were better developed than bottle-fed babies.

In another study, the medical records of 503 infants who were seen regularly at the baby clinic during their first year of life were examined. The advantages of breast-feeding over artificial feeding in reducing illness (middle ear infection, lower respiratory illness, diarrhoea, vomiting) were shown to operate independently of the effect of factors associated with illness such as socio-economic status, family size, day-care exposure, and birth-weight.

The beneficial effects of breast-milk cannot be measured – they are innumerable.

IV-1: *Nutritional Data Concerning Breast Milk*

Nutritive elements	Specific effects
Protein	• in less quantities than cow's milk • different quality, better adapted for the baby • more easily digested
Fat	• 7 to 8 times more essential fatty acids than cow's milk • maximizes brain development • more concentrated during the final minutes of feeding, which helps control a baby's appetite
Lactose or Sugar	• in greater quantities than in cow's milk • helps in brain development • fulfils a beneficial antidiuretic role to the mother • fosters, along with the bifidus factor, the growth of an intestinal flora which is resistant to infection
Iron	• absorbed five times better than from a milk formula

	• found in sufficient quantities in human milk
	• fights bacteria as well
Calcium	• contains less than cow's milk
Phosphorous	• sufficient amounts
	• easily absorbed by the baby
Sodium and	• contains three times less than cow's milk
Potassium	• better suited to baby's needs and
	• kidneys
Zinc	• present in the colostrum in great amounts
	• quantity well absorbed in breast-milk
Vitamin D	• present in small but *active* quantities in breast-milk
Vitamin C	• present in sufficient quantities
Vitamins A and B	• present in sufficient quantities
Vitamin E	• contains four times as much as cow's milk
	• is in good proportion with essential fatty acids.

C. *Protection Against Infections and Allergies*

It has long been noticed, in industrialized as well as in Third World countries, that breast-fed babies are less vulnerable to all kinds of infections than bottle-fed babies. We now understand how breast-fed babies acquire such resistance.

An infant is born with an incomplete immunological system. He is practically defenceless against his new, hostile environment. At this time breast-milk supplies a vast arsenal of protective agents which are transmitted primarily during the first days following birth through the colostrum. Each of the substances secreted in the colostrum and in human milk plays a precise self-defence role.

The Immunoglobulins Three immunoglobulins (or anti-bodies) are present in breast-milk. Two are definitely more active and are manufactured principally by the mammary glands themselves to satisfy the needs of the infant. Unaffected by the action of digestive substances or the stomach's acidity, they line the intestine with an antiseptic material and help the baby fight against bacteria, which cause diseases, including the polio virus.

The Bifidus Factor   A protective agent present in forty times greater amounts in the colostrum secreted in the few days after birth than in milk secreted a few weeks later, the bifidus factor permits the formation of an intestinal flora which resists infection and, by the same action, limits the multiplication of undesirable bacteria. The intestinal flora of the breast-fed baby is very different from that of the bottle-fed baby. Intestinal infections are practically non-existent in the first group.

Many other substances in breast milk help to complete the baby's defence system.

Anti-Allergenic Properties   Rates of infantile allergies are higher in countries where breast-feeding rates are low, and lower in populations where babies are breast-fed.

In the United States, many years ago, a study revealed that eczema, as well as other allergies, occured seven times more frequently in bottle-fed babies than in breast-fed babies.

The phenomenon is explained by the weak resistance of the baby's intestinal wall when confronted with protein not specific to the species. Breast-milk, on the other hand, supplies only specific human proteins and does not provoke an allergic reaction. Some doctors have succeeded in reducing the problems of allergies in infants from 40% to 7% by giving breast-milk exclusively during the first six months, and by removing dogs, cats, and dust from the immediate environment. This is why breast-milk is universally recognized as the best way of preventing allergies during infancy, especially in families whose histories reveal allergy problems.

Note: It can happen that a baby, breast-fed exclusively, will develop colic as well as skin eruptions. In the first instance, it seems that proteins found in *cow's milk consumed by the mother* are partially transmitted to the baby via the breast-milk, and when the mother adopts a diet which does not include cow's milk or beef, the baby stops having colic. In this particular instance, it is recommended that the mother drink a soya-based formula (Wysoy S-Formula) to eliminate the problem until the baby is able to tolerate the protein contained in cow's milk, at about six months of age. A dietetic consultation will provide appropriate readjustment of the maternal diet.

In the second instance, a baby of a few months of age, who suddenly develops dermatitis (severe skin irritation), might not be receiving enough zinc through breast-feeding, since the amount of zinc found in breast-milk can vary enormously from one mother to another. This can be corrected by adding foods rich in zinc to the maternal diet such as liver or wheat germ, and by applying a zinc-based ointment to the baby's skin.

D. A Source of Exceptional Contact

Breast-milk is not only a food which is marvellously well suited to the needs of the baby, as well as providing an anti-infection and anti-allergenic defence system, but it also permits the blossoming of a unique relationship between mother and child.

For several years now, the medical field has not only been trying to save lives and to assure average physical growth, but also has been looking at ways to foster favourable global development of the child. Part of this line of enquiry has been to look into the origin of the interaction between the newborn and his parents.

Struck by the high incidence of abandoned or abused children, and by the slow growth of children separated from their parents during the first months of life, these doctors have tried to discover a common element for these situations. During their research, they found a common denominator between the absence of physical contact between mother and child during the first days of life and a higher frequency of a number of problems.

The less often a mother took her child in her arms, the less eye contact and the less warmth there was between the two of them. Subsequently, more developmental and health problems occurred in the child.

The minutes and days following birth are key times to initiate and seal the mother-child relationship. Breast-feeding immediately after delivery, or within a few hours, permits establishment of this physical contact. The whole breast-feeding period reinforces this unique relationship.

It is undoubtedly possible to establish a happy mother-child relationship without breast-feeding one's child, but isn't breast-feeding the ideal way to do so?

Advantages for the Mother

The baby is without doubt the winner when it comes to breast-feeding, which is absolutely normal. However, the mother reaps some dividends as well. Before drawing up a list I would like to tell you about Mrs Thomas, a nurse in her sixties who is a health visitor. Mrs Thomas, who works with young mothers in her area, constantly tells her charges that breast-milk is perfect. Says Mrs Thomas:

'It is always at the proper temperature;
It is easily transported to a picnic;
It does not attract cats;
It comes in attractive containers!'

Mothers should truly realize the real benefits to themselves of breast-feeding.

A. A Source of Gratifying Exchanges

We have long minimized or simply ignored a newborn's reactions during the first days and months of life. Recent studies have revealed the mystery of the first hours of life, and the great awakening involved during the first hour following birth. The newborn baby follows human eye contact and reacts to the human voice; he is ready to nurse. Far from being passive, he interacts with his mother and participates in the blooming of a privileged relationship.

Nursing shortly after the birth of her child, at a time when the sucking reflex of the baby is at its maximum, helps the mother's uterus to contract, decreases the risks of haemorrhaging, and stimulates the production and secretion of milk. This early feeding seems to be associated with a longer and happier nursing period as well. According to studies conducted with new mothers in the UK, Sweden, and the United States, physical contact between mother and child immediately after birth promoted a longer nursing period than when there was no early contact.

Breast-feeding is not the only method of establishing this unique relationship, but it is such a natural process that it encourages faster adjustment between the child's and the mother's rhythms – a better synchronization between two beings.

B. Saving Time and Money

Breast-feeding simplifies a new mother's life, saves her money, and makes her daily routine all that more pleasurable. No need to buy milk formula, prepare bottles, care for rubber teats, wash containers, and so on. It implies a healthy and generous diet for the mother (see Chapter Six), but the price of the supplementary food required during the lactation period is much less than the cost of buying formula milk food.

IV-2: Daily Costs of Various Milk Preparations for Baby

A recent study comparing the costs of providing 852ml (30 oz) of breast-milk and various proprietary baby milks showed that breast milk, even allowing for the extra good foods in the mother's diet, costs half as much as powdered milk and as little as a third as much as convenient liquid milks.

The study did not take into account the extra costs involved in using sterilizing fluids and in providing new teats for feeding bottles.

C. Faster Weight Loss After Pregnancy

About 2 kg (4.5 lb.) of the weight gained during pregnancy is considered to be part of the maternal energy reserves required for breast-feeding. This additional weight is important since it is used in the production of maternal milk and thereby spares the mother's own vital reserves. It is, therefore, used during the nursing period and lost more rapidly when the mother breast-feeds. As a matter of fact, one study showed that at the end of three months a group of mothers who had breast-fed had lost an average of 1 kg (2.2 lb.) more than other mothers who had not breast-fed.

The Trend Towards Breast-Feeding

A survey involving obstetricians, and 1,000 mothers in 1976 who gave birth during the twenty-four previous months, was conducted throughout France. This survey clearly indicated an increase in breast-feeding in France between 1972 and 1976; 48% of mothers in 1976 breast-fed their child during their hospital stay.

In the UK and elsewhere

In 1980 53% of first time mothers were entirely breast-feeding their babies on discharge from hospital. In 1975 the figure for the corresponding group was 38%. The figures for breast-feeding among mothers of subsequent children are lower (44% in 1980 and 29% in 1975) but still the figures show an upward trend. In fact, in the last decade, a return to breast-feeding has been noticed in many industrialized countries. The trend is here to stay; note the phenomenal growth of breast feeding support groups organised by women themselves and of nationally known groups such as The National Childbirth Trust and La Leche League International.

CHAPTER FIVE

The Art of Breast-feeding

EVEN THOUGH breast-feeding is an ultranatural act, nursing is an art which is learned and has been traditionally transmitted from generation to generation. Since tradition was broken at the beginning of this century, two or three generations back, training is now done through a mid-wife, a health visitor, prenatal courses, or through the assistance of the National Childbirth Trust.

Breast-feeding essentially depends upon the instinctive reflex of the newborn associated with the maternal instinct, but this process has to be encouraged. In fact, more than 95% of women can breast-feed if they so desire. Unfortunately, certain myths often dispel this initial impetus and turn many parents away from this potentially enriching adventure. It is thus better to explain away these myths before continuing our discussion on the art of breast-feeding.

Answers to these Age-Old Myths

Breast-feeding does not alter the shape of the breasts

During pregnancy, the breasts increase in size and can change in shape long before the nursing period begins if a good supporting bra is not worn, or if the weight gained during pregnancy goes beyond the reasonable limit of 11 to 14 kg (24-30 lb). During the nursing period it is recommended that a proper brassiere be worn twenty-four hours a day, at least during the first few months, so that problems will not occur.

Breast-feeding does not promote weight gain

Certain studies have shown that nursing mothers lose one kilogram (2.2 lb.) more during the first three months following delivery than non-nursing mothers. Understandably, mothers who eat badly and too much, gain weight. Exercise also plays an important role in weight maintenance. If a nursing mother's physical activity is decreased considerably, her weight will vary in consequence.

Breast-feeding is not exhausting

It is a fact that during the first few days following delivery, the baby requires many feedings and much attention from the mother. However, as early as the second week, an improved feeding and sleeping rhythm is acquired by the baby.

In today's society where domestic help is not too common, the young mother has to temporarily forget about dust, fancy meals, and even telephone calls if she wants to keep up her physical and emotional strength! If she eats properly, reduces her usual activities during the first weeks, and if she takes naps whenever she feels the need, she'll readily adapt to the requirements of breast-feeding.

Breast-feeding allows the mother some freedom

Whatever the type of milk chosen, the infant requires a lot of attention and care during the first weeks of life. On the other hand, when milk production is regular and stabilized, towards the fourth or fifth week, the baby can take on occasion one bottle of formula or breast milk kept in the refrigerator or in the freezer (see page 49). When the father or a friend cares for the baby this bottle allows mother several hours of freedom each day, should she want it.

A baby fed breast-milk in a bottle during the first weeks gets used to drinking from a bottle and this helps in the transition period in later months.

The size of the breast — an inaccurate measure

There is no relationship between the initial breast size and the quantity of milk which will be produced and secreted by the mother. In reality, bigger breasts possess more fat, but not a larger milk reserve.

During pregnancy, the mammary gland network of each breast increases due to hormonal changes, and these 'little local milk manufacturers' are then responsible for milk production in both small and large breasts.

It is the mothers's relaxed attitude which seems to influence the quantity of milk secreted rather than breast size.

Breast-milk does not contain too much cholesterol

It is true that breast-milk contains more cholesterol than cow's milk or formula. Feared enemy of the adult over forty years of age, who is vulnerable to its effects, cholesterol, on the other hand, plays an important role in the development of the child's brain and nervous system. The new-born needs cholesterol.

At the end of the first year, after adopting the family's eating habits, there did not appear to be any difference in the blood cholesterol level of babies fed modified formulas during the first six months, and that of babies breast-fed over a similar length of time. Furthermore, the effect of a high or low-cholesterol diet on the cholesterol content of breast-milk has been verified. Whatever the mother's diet, cholesterol-rich or cholesterol-poor, breast-milk does not alter and consistently contains the same quantity of cholesterol. Nature knows best!

Breast-milk is not polluted

A few years ago the information media reported that PCBs – polychlorinated biphenyls – were found in Canadian, American and European mothers' breast-milk. These substances, which have been used in industry since the 1930s, are carefully monitored in the UK. They are used in electrical machinery, for example in capacitors and heat exchangers, and it used to be possible for small amounts to be discharged as effluent into our rivers. However the Department of the Environment now imposes strict rules for the disposal of these substances. In many factories PCBs are being phased out, and in 1971 the sole manufacturers agreed voluntarily to restrict their use to close applications, that is in sealed units from which the substances can not escape.

No research has irrefutably proved that PCBs are responsible for any specific illness, but they are substances which, if released into the environment, enter the food chain. They are found to accumulate in the adipose, or fatty tissue, in the body and may, under certain conditions of stress or malnutrition, impede the function of the liver. However, in the UK there seems to be little risk of contamination because of the strict rules governing the use of PCBs and because the Ministry of Agriculture, Food and Fisheries constantly monitors all food sources for harmful elements.

Not all mothers can breast-feed

Even if more than 95% of mothers are physically able to breast-feed, a mother who does not want to breast-feed should not do so. In actual fact, there are only a very few absolute medical contraindications which can prevent a mother from breast-feeding. In such cases, the treating physician or specialist is the best counsel.

A badly nourished mother can nonetheless breast-feed

The mother's diet does not influence the principal nutrients contained in breast-milk. Only the volume of milk will decrease in extreme cases of malnutrition. In developing countries, where the mother's diet is often far from sufficient, breast-milk supplies adequate quantities of protein, fat, sugar, and immunological substances during the first three months, although the mineral and vitamin content may be low. In spite of these inadequacies, breast-milk from poorly nourished women is able to assure the growth and initial development of millions of children throughout the world.

A decision which should be made together

In our society, the art of breast-feeding can hardly be improvised at the last minute, after the baby is born.

Even if it is impossible to dispute the superiority of breast-milk, the decision made to breast-feed involves a certain amount of reflection. It is a decision that should be made after serious thinking throughout the pregnancy and even before. It is a joint decision made between husband and wife, to be discussed by the family if other children are involved since breast-feeding alters the family routine somewhat during the first months.

The husband's approval and encouragement should not be underestimated as his overall attitude largely contributes to the mother's calm and serenity. A father's tense or contrary attitude can adversely affect the mother's spirits and could decrease milk production.

Once the decision to breast-feed is made, an exemplary doctor encourages the prospective parents, and supplies information necessary to successful breast-feeding.

Before birth, the physical conditioning of the breast is an adjunct or addition to the psychological preparation of the couple.

Conditioning the Breasts before Delivery

To facilitate the first feeding and increase the elasticity of the nipples, it is recommended that the breasts be carefully prepared during the last trimester of pregnancy. Only a few minutes per day are required. It is simply necessary to:
1. Rub the nipples for a few minutes twice a day with a rough bath towel; or

2. Strengthen the nipple by pulling on it with two fingers, the forefinger and the thumb. The nipples will then lengthen easily and will provide better secretion of the milk after birth. (The extending of the nipple can provoke a slight secretion of a yellowish liquid, colostrum, the forerunner of real breast-milk. This secretion is perfectly normal. By washing the nipple as indicated below, there is absolutely no problem.)
3. Wash the nipples daily with warm water: this prevents the irritation and drying of the nipples which can be caused by the secretions.
4. A lanoline-based cream can be applied to the nipples to prevent irritation and dryness.

While at the hospital:
- During delivery, avoid as much as possible the use of sedatives, since their use decreases the baby's reflexes at birth.
- As soon as the baby is born, he/she should be breast-fed, since it is during this first hour of life that the baby's sucking reflex is at its maximum. This early sucking activates the mechanism for the production of breast-milk.
- It is preferable that the baby 'ward-in' to allow feeding on demand. During the first days which are days of learning and adaptation, the feedings should be numerous, as many as ten the first day. This will stimulate production and secretion of the milk and satisfy the baby's need for warmth and tenderness.
- Find the most comfortable nursing position with the help of a nurse. Nurse no more than five minutes at each breast during each feeding on the first day. Offer both breasts at each feeding starting with the breast offered last at the preceding feeding.
- Gradually increase the length of each feeding each day.
- Never interrupt the baby while he is actively feeding to burp him – wait until he pauses. This will enable him to reject the bubbles he has swallowed.
- Never give the baby a bottle of formula or sweetened water between feedings. This decreases the baby's appe-

tite and disrupts the still fragile milk production process.

- During the entire lactation period, support the breasts with a good-quality cotton nursing brassiere which opens to adequately expose a large part of the breast, not only the nipple. Avoid use of plastic or rubber-lined brassieres which irritate the nipples because they trap excess moisture.

The Art of Nursing on Demand

Following a number of personal accounts and a conversation with a National Childbirth Trust member, I became convinced of the importance of nursing on demand, without a fixed timetable. At first, this arrangement seems to require the mother to be available at all times but, as the weeks pass, mother and child comply to a jointly satisfactory rhythm and, when the needs of the newborn are considered during the first days of life, the benefits of such an arrangement are widely appreciated.

During the first hours of life, the child is wide-awake and is actively discovering his new environment. He reacts to this environment. His sucking reflex is particularly well developed during the first few minutes after delivery. As mentioned previously, during the first twenty-four hours of life the baby should nurse as many as ten times and perhaps even more. The mother who can respond to the appetite requirements of the baby by having him 'ward-in' satisfies her baby while helping herself, since these small but numerous feedings initiate a good milk supply. A number of studies associate part of the success of breast-feeding with the first feeding, given immediately after delivery or within the first hours of the infant's life. Other observations conclude that the baby who is close to his mother from the start finds an acceptable biorythm more rapidly, and his nursing and sleeping schedules are spaced more regularly.

The great awakening of the first hours now over, the baby falls into a deep sleep, and more intense cries are heard only around the third day. This ritual peculiar to the newborn entails that the mother be initially alert and available, but underlines as well the necessity to abandon a fixed nursing schedule at three- or four-hour intervals during this key period.

Gradually the baby is able to take larger and larger quantities of milk at one time, and his digestive system is also better adapted. At the end of a few weeks, he normally acquires a certain regularity and three or four hours can lapse between feedings. He can often sleep six consecutive hours between two feedings, once every twenty-four hours . . .Blessed are parents whose baby chooses the night for this prolonged nap!

As the entire breast-feeding process is an interaction between mother and child, after a few weeks the two adapt to a satisfactory way of living, without a rigid schedule.

One small precautionary message regarding breast-feeding on demand: interpretation of the baby's crying is very important, since crying does not always signal hunger. To feed a baby at the least bit of crying can involve serious long-term consequences.

A compromise between total feeding on demand and the fixed schedule seems to me to be acceptable after the first few weeks in order to respect the physical needs of the child as well as the psychological needs of the mother.

This compromise implies that certain feedings are given at more or less regular intervals during the day (10 o'clock, 1 o'clock, 4 o'clock, and 7 o'clock). The others (the first feeding in the morning and the last feeding of the evening) are given according to the baby's requests. This schedule should be flexible and comprehensive. If the baby is sleeping soundly at 1 o'clock, he can be fed at 1.30, and the following feeding is given at 4.30pm rather than at 4pm.

To each her own schedule . . . A happy mother is twice as valuable.

Problem Areas and Solutions

It goes without saying that the return home requires further adaptation on the part of the mother and her infant. Four or five days after delivery, milk production is not yet stabilized, and learning about breast-feeding is still continuing. The nights are short and the days long . . . sometimes there are problems, but they are rarely without a solution.

Breast congestion

Breast congestion, or engorgement, can occur at the beginning of the breast-feeding regimen if the breasts are not completely emptied after each nursing or if the feedings are too far apart. A hot-water compress quickly relieves the engorged breast. A breast which is too full leaves little of the nipple for the baby to suck on. In order to enable him to drink easily, it is suggested that milk be manually expressed before or after nursing.

Cracked, fissured, or split nipples

Nipples can crack, fissure or split, particularly in women with delicate, pale skin, in spite of proper preparation of the breasts during pregnancy. To reduce discomfort, a lanolin-based cream is applied on the nipple and nursing is limited to five to seven minutes per nipple at each feeding for a few days. After each nursing period, the nipple is dried and left exposed to the air for a fifteen-minute period.

Breast infection or mastitis

Breast infection is usually present when the mother complains that she is really exhausted, has painful breasts, and a fever. Rest is the best medicine, as well as frequent breast-feeding which will decongest the breast. Should the fever persist, the doctor can prescribe antibiotics which will not prevent the continuation of breast-feeding.

Insufficient milk

An insufficient supply of milk is without a doubt the greatest source of worry and one of the main causes of the premature abandonment of breast-feeding. This milk shortage, usually short-lived, is ordinarily associated with fatigue, anxiety, or a greater demand by the baby caused by a growth spurt. When one realizes that nursing mothers of twins are well able to provide for their babies, confidence in a mother's ability to nurse one child is quickly regained. On the other hand, we should realize that if the nursing mother reduces her food consumption, thinking that she will be able to lose weight faster, she can involuntarily decrease her milk supply considerably.

Rest, an adequate diet (see Chapter Six), a refreshing shower or a warm relaxing bath before breast-feeding, accompanied occasionally by a small glass of wine or beer, are but a few ways to restore confidence and relaxation in the temporarily distressed nursing mother.

Another method of increasing milk production is by increasing the number of feedings for a few days which stimulates milk production and better corresponds to the increased appetite needs of the baby.

Freezing Breast-Milk

The freezing of breast-milk has long been carried on by milk-bank organizations responsible for preserving this precious liquid, donated by nursing mothers in various regions in order to supply milk for premature, hospitalized, or ailing babies.

However, the home-freezing of breast-milk is a relatively new development. It is a simple technique and, while it remains one of the most efficient in food preservation, it is one which is widely available to everyone. Thanks to the home-freezing of breast-milk, more freedom is available to the mother and it enables the father to feed his baby without the child having to change his high-quality diet. This also permits the mother of a hospitalized premature baby to provide at a distance for his nutritive and immunological needs.

It is recommended that the milk be manually expressed. Certain hygienic rules should be observed in order to avoid contaminating the breast-milk. Let us proceed by stages:

1. Generously pour boiling water into a pyrex measuring cup or other container to be used for the milk. Leave it for two to three minutes in order to sterilize it, then pour out.
2. Prepare a small feeding bottle (the type with a screw-on cap), and label the date of collection with a self-adherent tag.
3. Before extracting the milk, wash hands and nipples.
4. Gently massage the breast and the nipple in order to stimulate the let down reflex.
5. Express the milk by placing the thumb and forefinger around the nipple – at first, this may take some time, but with practice, several ounces can be expressed in about fifteen minutes.
6. Pour the milk from the sterilized collecting cup into the feeding bottle.
7. Seal the bottle well and refrigerate immediately.
8. Once the bottle of milk has cooled, after about an hour in the refrigerator, place it in the rear of the freezer, away from the door, in order to ensure that the temperature is very cold and uniform. In the refrigerator, breast-milk can keep for a maximum of two days; in the freezer, breast-milk may be kept for two to six months.
9. To warm the milk, take out from the freezer and place the bottle in a container of warm water for about five minutes. Shake the milk to evenly distribute the fat particles and serve at once.
10. Once thawed, but not warmed, breast-milk can be kept in the refrigerator for one day.

Length of Breast-Feeding Period

Health professionals agree that breast-milk suffices by itself in adequately providing for the nutritive needs of the baby for the first four to six months of life, as long as the baby is born at term, is of normal weight, and in good health.

No one limits the breast-feeding period to six months; breast-milk can complement the baby's diet for several years, should the mother desire to do so. We simply emphasize that the maximum contribution of breast-milk as the only item in a baby's diet is during the first four to six months of life.

In reality, the duration of the breast-feeding period, whether two weeks, one month or two, does not matter; the experience is worthwhile for both parties, mother and child. Breast-milk is still the most marvellously well-adapted food for baby and the most readily accessible for the mother. Results of a survey conducted in the UK in 1980 by Martin and Monk on behalf of the DHSS revealed that 26% of infants are still breast-fed at four months of age, 22% at six months and 12% at nine months. Many are the mothers, whose experiences have not been statistically recorded and who have successfully breast-fed for six months, who have taken time to write to me of their success.

Thanks to the advantage of freezing a reserve of breast-milk as soon as milk production is adequate to do so, breast-feeding can become compatible with a flexible work schedule after about three months.

Weaning is a sensitive time to go through. Ideally this transition period is a gentle one, slow and gradual, with little upset for both baby and mother.

If the child is six or seven months old, he gradually leaves the breast and adapts to a cup containing whole-milk or formula. If the baby is only a few weeks or months old, he gradually gives up breast-milk for formula. Three weeks should be allowed for the change.

One method is to substitute one bottle-feeding for one breast-feeding every four or five days, keeping the morning and night feeding at the breast. Let go of the morning nursing before the night one. By decreasing the number of breast-feeding periods, milk production is automatically reduced and the mother's adaptation period is facilitated.

Another method involves reducing each feeding by five minutes, that is two and a half minutes per breast. Feeding is then completed by giving three ounces of formula in a bottle. Five days after the first decrease, the length of the nursing period is again cut by five minutes, and four ounces of formula is offered after nursing. The process is continued until the formula entirely replaces breast-milk.

To obtain additional information about breast-feeding, the following books are available:

1. *The Womanly Art of Breastfeeding*
   La Leche League International, 3rd edition, 1981
2. *The Breast Feeding Book*
   Maire Messenger
   Century Publishing 1982
3. *The Experience of Breastfeeding*
   Sheila Kitzinger
   Pelican, Penguin

CHAPTER SIX

The Nursing Mother's Diet

THANKS TO THE efficient work of the mammary glands and the mother's adequate diet, a breast-fed baby receives the ideal food in terms of both quality and quantity.

After thorough examination of the composition of breast-milk in Chapter Four, we can now turn our attention to the diet of the producer who is responsible for the production of this 'super' baby food. It is important to stress that the mother's diet influences not only the quality, but also the quantity of milk secreted by the mammary glands. As previously stated, however, breast-milk cannot be *significantly* altered in quality or quantity except in extreme cases of malnutrition. In fact, even in developing countries nursing mothers are able to produce milk which contains sufficient amounts of protein, fat, and lactose (sugar) during the first few months following delivery. When there is severe malnutrition, it is the quantity of the milk which is insufficient, not the essential ingredients.

However, in most situations a nursing mother who eats well produces milk which is richer in vitamins than milk produced by a mother who is malnourished. Moreover, the well-fed mother does not endanger her own reserves, a fact which should not be understated.

This said, the nursing mother's diet is not complicated. It is made up of the same good foods which were found to be so important during pregnancy (Chapter Three), but in slightly larger quantities.

150-200 More Calories

The nutritive needs of the newborn are greater than during his fetal life. The caloric intake in the nursing mother's diet should, therefore, be slightly higher than during her pregnancy if she wants to manufacture sufficient quantities of milk. In relation to the energy demands during pregnancy, an *additional* daily supplement of 300 kilocalories is required; this represents an increase of 500 kilocalories in the diet of the nursing mother since she became pregnant. This caloric surplus seems like a small amount to supply 16 to 30 ounces (480 to 825 ml) of milk per day, but this is not the only source of calories.

The 4.4 to 6.6 pounds of fat deposits (2 to 3 kilos), or more, deposited in the maternal organism during the gestation period and kept throughout the delivery period, are used at a rate of about 300 calories per day as an additional source of energy. Slowly but surely, these fat deposits disappear, used for the benefit of the baby during the first three or four months.

A daily diet containing between 2,200 to 2,500 calories seems to satisfy both mother's and baby's needs. This can be even more generous depending on the mother's dietary habits and her level of physical activity.

Key Foods Found on the Daily Menu

The suggested portions for each food group represent the *minimum* quantities capable of satisfying the nutritive needs of a well-fed woman before and during pregnancy.

Milk Products

Without a doubt, milk products represent a food group which is particularly essential to mother and child during the nursing period. A litre (2 pints) of milk per day or its equivalent in milk products is the minimum daily amount required to supply all the calcium needed for tooth and bone formation in the baby, while still conserving the mother's own reserves. As a complementary contribution, a litre (2 pints) of milk supplies more than 32-35 grams of complete protein, a good quantity of B vitamins, and the entire daily calcium requirement. Vitamin D enriched milk may be bought in concentrated form in tins.

An eight-ounce glass of milk (250 ml) can be replaced by:

1½ oz. (45 gm) of cheese

or

8 oz. (240 gm) of yogurt

or

8 oz. (250 ml) of milk-based soup or dessert

or

2 scoops of ice cream or low fat ice-cream (occasionally)

Meat, Poultry, Fish, or Substitute

One daily serving of 4 to 4½ oz. of meat, poultry, or fish is ample in supplying a sufficient quantity of protein, B vitamins and iron.

A weekly meal of liver, kidney, or heart supplies an additional amount of iron and zinc, useful nutritive elements needed by the nursing mother.

One or more cups of cooked dried vegetables (soya beans, dried peas, lentils, etc.) supplies the vegetarian nursing mother with good quality vegetable protein which becomes even more effective in building and repairing tissues if eaten with whole-grain cereal or bread.

Eggs

Four to seven eggs a week are recommended for the nursing mother. Two can replace a serving of meat. Eggs contain easily assimilated protein and supply vitamins and minerals. Their contribution should not be underestimated, nor should they be eliminated from the menu because of their high cholesterol content. According to many researchers studying atherosclerosis, it is the total quantity of saturated fats which affects the cholesterol level in the blood. Instead of eliminating eggs entirely from the diet, it would be better to watch the portions of meat, cheese, butter or margarine.

Whole-grain Cereal and Bread

The 'carnivorous' nursing mother should eat four to six slices of whole-grain bread or its equivalent in cereal products every day. Bread not only rounds off the total number of calories, but supplies a significant quantity of protein, iron, and B vitamins.

The vegetarian nursing mother should eat six to eight portions of bread or cereal products every day in order to complete the pulse protein and to supply additional iron, B vitamins, and calories.

A slice of whole-grain bread can be replaced by:
one bowl of whole-grain cereal, cooked or ready-to-eat
or
½ cup (125 ml) or brown of parboiled rice
or
½ cup (125 ml) of enriched pastas
or
one whole-wheat or bran roll
or
one whole-wheat, buckwheat or oatmeal pancake.

Fruit

Overflowing with vitamins, minerals, food fibre and permissible sugar, fruits play an appealing role in the nursing mother's diet. They supply colour and flavour without tilting the scales the wrong way. Two portions per day represent a *minimum* amount.

Whether fresh, frozen, or canned, fruits are a winning part of any meal. Several kinds of fruit are now available, and canned without sugar or canned in unsweetened fruit juice represent valid choices when fresh fruit is too expensive.

Fruits rich in vitamin C, such as oranges, grapefruits, strawberries, and melons, should be eaten every day and are a welcome addition to a vegetarian diet based on cereals or pulses, since they enhance iron absorption.

It is well known that iron is an important nutrient in the proper functioning of the organism. As all precious substances seem to be, however, iron is especially vulnerable particularly in a meatless diet. Since vitamin C can increase the absorption of iron from foods, notably vegetables, consumption of fruit and vegetables at each meal is very beneficial in a vegetarian diet.

Vegetables

A food without fault which contains a great number of nutrients and few calories, yellow, green, red or white, cooked or raw, in juice or in soup form, all vegetables add colour and texture to our meals. Whether they are fresh, frozen, or canned, they contribute to the daily nutritional food balance.

Three servings per day represent minimum rations. Additional supplementary portions are always an added health benefit.

Fats

A moderate quantity of butter, margarine that has been only partially hydrogenated, or polyunsaturated oil (corn, sunflower, etc.) complete the menu. Used in moderation for cooking, as a spread or as a dressing, fats add useful calories while aiding in the absorption of several vitamins.

A diet which contains a larger amount of polyunsaturated fats than saturated fats has a parallel influence on breast-milk. Vegetarian nursing mothers who consume neither milk products, meat, nor eggs, produce milk which is richer in polyunsaturated fats than 'carnivorous' nursing mothers.

A nursing mother need not adopt such an extreme diet, however, since human milk naturally contains an appreciable amount of unsaturated fats, as much as five times more than cow's milk.

Breast-milk resists reflecting fluctuations in the intake of cholesterol in the nursing mother's diet. Whether the diet be high or low in cholesterol, the amount of cholesterol in breast-milk remains relatively stable, responding to nature's requirements and actively working at developing the baby's brain and nervous system.

Liquids

Contrary to popular belief, liquids consumed by a mother do not directly influence breast-milk production. As a baby is the first to be 'served,' it is the mother who runs the risk of suffering from an insufficient amount of liquids and becoming dehydrated.

If milk products are consumed in the form of liquid milk, if one of the day's fruits is taken in juice form, and if soup or vegetable juice is added to the menu, a few glasses of water are all that remain to be taken each day.

However, if foods are eaten mainly in solid form (cheese, stewed fruits, or cooked vegetables), it will then be necessary to drink several glasses of water between and at meals in order to maintain the water reserves essential to the proper functioning of the maternal organism.

Sweets, Pastries, and Others

If one wishes to give priority to the key food elements useful to both the mother and the baby during this crucial period, and if at the same time one wants to avoid consumption of useless calories, there then remains little place for sweets, pastries, and other such foods. To occasionally indulge is permissible; however, to regularly consume foods high in sugar and empty-calories (sweets, soft drinks, cakes) is not recommended.

Eating Four or Five Times Daily

In order to eat all the foods previously recommended daily, a mother should eat more often by adding some sensible snacks made up of milk products and fresh or even dried fruit.

Digestion is thus facilitated, absorption is improved, and the quantities consumed at mealtime remain at a reasonable level. Small snacks are a source of energy which enable a mother to take well-deserved pauses and rest periods during the day.

Problem Foods or Fluids

In reality, very few foods or fluids can seriously harm the mother or the child during the lactation period. However:

- Some may cause digestive problems in the nursing mother such as fried foods and foods which are too rich or too sweet, but these, in any case, are hardly advisable for anyone.

- Strong-tasting vegetables such as cabbage, onions, or garlic can alter the taste of breast-milk, but few babies object to this variation. It is better to experiment and see how a baby reacts to these vegetables rather than to completely eliminate them.

- Very spicy and salty foods also alter the taste of breast-milk. However, generally speaking, no one should over-indulge in these foods, least of all nursing mothers.

- Chocolate's deservedly bad reputation is probably valid since certain unfortunate reactions have been noticed in babies whose mothers ate chocolate in large amounts (constipation, eczema, irritability, wakefulness). Here, as elsewhere, the 'quantity and frequency' factor should be considered. It is not the occasional small piece of chocolate which is to blame, but rather the daily chocolate bar and the regular eating of other chocolate or cocoa products.

- Fresh-water fish (salmon, pike, trout, bass), are safe to eat as long as they come from rivers which are not contaminated by industrial and urban effluent. Seafoods (cod, sole, haddock, plaice, halibut) do not present any problem and can be eaten liberally and frequently by the nursing mother.

- Coffee and tea stimulate the mother and can over stimulate the baby if they are consumed in great amounts. Moderation is beneficial in many situations, for both mother and child.
- Alcohol is rapidly assimilated in breast-milk and can harm the baby if consumed in large quantities. On the other hand, the occasional glass of wine or beer is often recommended by paediatricians as a source of relaxation and fluid consumption for the mother.

Supplements: Essential or Superfluous?

As stated in the chapter about pregnancy, a nursing mother does not, in principle, require vitamin or mineral supplements. But, in actual fact, a high percentage of nursing mothers continue to use prenatal supplements during the nursing period.

When the effect of taking these supplements is evaluated, with regard to the nutrient composition of the breast-milk and the maternal reserves of well-nourished mothers, there is no appreciable difference between mothers who take supplements and those who do not. It should be remembered that we are discussing properly fed mothers – the solution rests in what a mother eats.

- Even if a mother drinks two large glasses of milk per day, a daily supplement of 10 μg of vitamin D in liquid or tablet form is necessary in order to make full use of the calcium found in milk. (Liquid cows' milk contains only a trace of vitamin D. In the UK vitamin D enriched milk is available, in concentrated form, in tins, as evaporated milk.)
- If a mother does not incorporate a sufficient amount of milk products in her diet, that is, the equivalent of a litre (2 pints) of milk in the form of cheese, yogurt, or milk-based dishes, she must add a calcium supplement in order to reach 1,200 mg of calcium per day. Otherwise

she will lose calcium from her own bones.

- If a mother is a strict vegetarian, that is, she does not eat any meat, milk products, or eggs, she should take supplements of vitamin B^{12}, calcium, and vitamin D in order not to damage the baby's growth or development.

Daily needs:
B^{12} – no figures stated in UK but $5\mu g$ in US *
1,200 mg of calcium
10 μg of vitamin D

- If the mother's diet is definitely insufficient, she should continue the daily use of prenatal supplements until her diet improves.

Pay Close Attention to Using Medication

The baby receives, in spite of himself, everything that a mother eats: food, liquids, medication, or drugs. A magic filter which allows only the good substances to enter the mammary glands from the maternal blood does not exist. Everything is transmitted to the baby and can affect his incomplete digestive and renal system.

All medication taken by the mother is thus passed in small amounts into the breast-milk. Most have little effect on the child, but some, such as anticoagulants, hypothyroids, amphetamines, and diuretics, must be avoided. The use of the birth-control pill during the lactation period is still quite controversial since it reduces the quantity of the breast-milk and leaves traces of hormones. If absolutely necessary, a minimal dose prescribed by a consulting physician, and containing progesterone only, seems preferable.

As a general guideline concerning medication, abstinence is desirable when possible. In case of necessity, a treating physician should be consulted.

---

*Note: The amounts of nutrients suggested by the Department of Health and Social Security may slightly differ from the ones put forward by Health Authorities in other countries.

Menu-Planning

In order to make use of the recommendations contained in this chapter, the following pages present seven complete menus for 'carnivorous' nursing mothers, and seven complete menus adapted for 'lacto-ovo vegetarian' nursing mothers. The nutritive value of the menus is then analysed.

Menus for Nursing Mothers

With Meat	Vegetarian
DAY 1	**DAY 1**
BREAKFAST	BREAKFAST
½ grapefruit	½ grapefruit
banana bread with ricotta or cottage cheese (¼ cup or 60 ml)	banana bread with ricotta or cottage cheese (¼ cup or 60 ml)
glass of milk or milky coffee (8 oz. or 250 ml)	glass of milk or milky coffee (8 oz. or 250 ml)
LUNCH	LUNCH
raw vegetables	raw vegetables
lentil soup (1 cup or 250 ml)	lentil soup (1 cup or 250 ml)
whole-wheat bread (2 slices)	whole-wheat bread (2 slices)
plain yogurt with fresh or canned peaches (4 oz. or 125 ml)	plain yogurt with fresh or canned peaches (4 oz. or 125 ml)
fruit and milk (8 oz. or 250 ml)	fruit and milk (8 oz. or 250 ml)
DINNER	DINNER
baked chicken (3 oz. or 90 gm)	oven-baked vegetable casserole
brown rice	herb bread
carrots and green beans	salad greens
baked apple	baked apple
herbal tea	herbal tea
milk or yogurt (8 oz. or 250 ml)	milk or yogurt (8 oz. or 250 ml)
DAY 2	**DAY 2**
BREAKFAST	BREAKFAST
orange juice	orange juice

oatmeal with raisins and milk
whole-wheat bread, toasted
  (1 slice)
milk or milky coffee
  (6 oz. or 180 ml)

LUNCH

raw vegetables
grilled salmon sandwich or pita
  bread stuffed with salmon
banana
glass of milk (8 oz. or 250 ml)
fruit juice and cheese (1½ oz.
  45 gm)

DINNER

lentil and brown-rice casserole
courgettes and carrots
ginger and melon yogurt
  (4 oz. or 125 ml)
herbal tea
milk of yogurt (8 oz.)

oatmeal with raisins and milk
whole-wheat bread, toasted
  (1 slice)
milk or milky coffee
  (6 oz. or 180 ml)

LUNCH

raw vegetables
one wholemeal roll spread
  with peanut butter or cheese
banana
glass of milk (8 oz. or 250 ml)
fruit juice and cheese (1½ oz.
  or 45 gm)

DINNER

lentil and brown-rice casserole
courgettes and carrots
ginger and melon yogurt
  (4 oz. or 125 ml)
herbal tea
milk or yogurt (8 oz.)

DAY 3

BREAKFAST

quartered orange
egg (hard-boiled
  or poached)
whole-wheat bread, toasted
  (2 slices)
milk or milky coffee (8 oz. or
  250 ml)

LUNCH

salad of cooked and raw
  vegetables
cheese cubes (2 oz. or 60 gm)
  and nuts
slice of whole-wheat bread or
  bran roll
fresh or canned pears
milk
milk and dried fruits (8 oz. or
  250 ml)

DAY 3

BREAKFAST

quartered orange
egg (hard-boiled
  or poached)
whole-wheat bread, toasted
  (2 slices)
milk or milky coffee (8 oz. or
  250 ml)

LUNCH

salad of cooked and raw
  vegetables
cheese cubes (2 oz. or 60 gm)
  and nuts
slice of whole-wheat bread or
  bran roll
fresh or canned pears
milk
milk and dried fruits (8 oz. or
  250 ml)

DINNER

pot roast (3 oz. or 90 gm)
coleslaw with apples
slice of whole-wheat bread
fresh fruit cocktail

herbal tea or water
milk or yogurt (8 oz. or
    250 ml)

DINNER

red kidney beans (1 cup or
    250 ml) with herbs and rice
    (½ cup or 125 ml)
coleslaw with apples
slice of whole-wheat bread
fresh fruit cocktail
herbal tea or water
milk or yogurt (8 oz. or
    250 ml)

DAY 4

BREAKFAST

½ grapefruit
shredded wheat cereal with
    milk garnished with nuts
    and wheat germ
slice of whole-wheat bread,
    toasted
milk or milky coffee (6 oz.
    or 180 ml)

LUNCH

vegetable juice or soup
chopped egg sandwich (1 egg
    on slice of whole-wheat
    bread)
apple sauce
milk (8 oz. or 250 ml)
apple and cheese cube (1½ oz.
    or 45 gm)

DINNER

poached fish fillet (4 oz. or
    120 gm)
baked potato
plain broccoli
banana with yogurt sauce
    (4 oz. or 125 ml)
herbal tea
milk or yogurt (8 oz. or
    250 ml)

DAY 4

BREAKFAST

½ grapefruit
shredded wheat cereal with
    milk garnished with nuts
    and wheat germ
slice of whole-wheat bread,
    toasted
milk or milky coffee (6 oz.
    or 180 ml)

LUNCH

vegetable juice or soup
chopped egg sandwich (1 egg
    on slice of whole-wheat
    bread)
apple sauce
milk (8 oz. or 250 ml)
apple and cheese cube (1½ oz.
    or 45 gm)

DINNER

stuffed vegetable crêpes au
    gratin
salad greens

banana with yogurt sauce
    (4 oz. or 125 ml)
herbal tea
milk or yogurt (8 oz. or
    250 ml)

DAY 5

BREAKFAST

orange juice
1 poached or hard-boiled egg
2 slices of whole-wheat bread,
    toasted
milk or milky coffee (8 oz.
    or 250 ml)

LUNCH

cream of green vegetable soup
Cos lettuce salad with
    beans (1 cup)
2 slices whole-wheat bread
yogurt with fresh or canned
    peaches (4 oz. or 125 ml)
milk (8 oz. or 250 ml)
raisins and milk (8 oz. or
    250 ml)

DINNER

beef liver creole (3 oz. or
    90 gm)
brown rice with parsley (1 cup
    or 250 ml)
french green beans
apple sauce
herbal tea
milk or yogurt (8 oz. or
    250 ml)

DAY 6

BREAKFAST

apple juice
shredded wheat sprinkled with
    nuts, raisins and milk
1 slice whole-wheat bread
    toasted or 1 bran roll
milk or milky coffee (6 oz. or
    180 ml)

LUNCH

raw vegetables
grilled cheese (2 oz. or 60 gm)
    sandwich with tomato

DAY 5

BREAKFAST

orange juice
1 poached or hard-boiled egg
2 slices whole-wheat bread,
    toasted
milk or milky coffee (8 oz.
    or 250 ml)

LUNCH

cream of green vegetable soup
Cos lettuce salad with
    beans (1 cup)
2 slices whole-wheat bread
yogurt with fresh or canned
    peaches (4 oz. or 125 ml)
milk (8 oz. or 250 ml)
raisins and milk (8 oz. or
    250 ml)

DINNER

vegetable juice
vegetable pizza with lots of
    cheese
chinese cabbage salad

apple sauce
herbal tea
milk or yogurt (8 oz. or
    250 ml)

DAY 6

BREAKFAST

apple juice
shredded wheat sprinkled with
    nuts, raisins and milk
1 slice whole-wheat bread
    toasted or 1 bran roll
milk or milky coffee (6 oz. or
    180 ml)

LUNCH

raw vegetables
grilled cheese (2 oz. or 60 gm)
    sandwich with tomato

apple or pear
milk (8 oz. or 250 ml)
fruit and milk (4 oz. or 125 ml)

braised beef with parslied
  noodles
1 slice whole-wheat bread
lettuce-and-spinach salad
yogurt (4 oz. or 125 ml) and
  strawberries
herbal tea
milk (4 oz. or 125 ml)

apple or pear
milk (8 oz. or 250 ml)
fruit and milk (4 oz. or 125 ml)

DINNER

baked beans with grated cheese
parslied rice
1 slice whole-wheat bread
lettuce-and-spinach salad
yogurt (4 oz. or 125 ml) and
  strawberries
herbal tea
milk (4 oz. or 125 ml)

DAY 7

BREAKFAST

quartered orange
1 oz. (30 gm) cheese
2 bran rolls
milk or milky coffee (8 oz. or
  250 ml)

LUNCH

vegetable juice or broth
chicken and rice salad

1 slice whole-wheat bread
banana with plain yogurt
  (4 oz. or 125 ml)
milk (8 oz. or 250 ml)
raisins and nuts
milk (8 oz. or 250 ml)

DINNER

cheese omelette (2 eggs)
chinese cabbage salad
2 slices whole-wheat bread
baked apple
oatmeal biscuit (1)
herbal tea
milk or yogurt (4 oz. or
  125 ml)

DAY 7

BREAKFAST

quartered orange
1 oz. (30 gm) cheese
2 bran rolls
milk or milky coffee (8 oz. or
  250 ml)

LUNCH

raw vegetables
lentil or pea soup (1 cup or
  250 ml)
2 slices whole-wheat bread
banana and plain yogurt
  (4 oz. or 125 ml)
milk (8 oz. or 250 ml)
raisins and nuts
milk (8 oz. or 250 ml)

DINNER

cheese omelette (2 eggs)
chinese cabbage salad
2 slices whole-wheat bread
baked apple
oatmeal biscuit (1)
herbal tea
milk or yogurt (4 oz. or
  125 ml)

VI-1: *Nutritive Values of the 7 Menus for Nursing Mothers*

A. *Meat Menus (4 to 4½ oz. (125-135 gm) of poultry, meat, or fish per day)*

Menus	Calories	Protein (g)	Calcium (mg)	Iron (mg)	Vit. B12 (µg)	Vit.C (mg)
Day 1	1985	104	1556	16	5	213
Day 2	2415	97	2119	15	10	251
Day 3	2367	104	2074	17	10	322
Day 4	1800	102	1858	14	7	159
Day 5	2192	114	2253	22[3]	78[3]	297
Day 6	2138	95	1968	18	6	219
Day 7	2194	105	2020	18	7	193
DAILY AVERAGE	2156[1]	103[2]	1978	17	18	236[4]
Quantities Recommended:						
UK	2700	68	1200	15	no rec. fig.	60

1 The average caloric content is below that recommended by the Department of Health and Social Security but approaches the actual quantities consumed by nursing mothers. Furthermore, the amounts shown do not include the fats normally used in cooking and as spreads except those used for dressings. In most cases, semi-skimmed milk and plain yogurt are used. It would, therefore, be easy to adjust the calories contained in this diet if so desired.

2. Regardless of the fact that the meat, poultry, and fish portions are small, the menus contain much more protein than recommended.

3. Day 5 menu is very rich in iron and vitamin B12 because it contains liver, a food super-rich in both these nutrients.

4. A high amount of vitamin C contained in these diets reflects a high fruit and vegetable content. This also implies that vitamin supplements are unnecessary when one eats properly.

5. Iron needs during lactation are not substantially different

from those of non-pregnant women, but continued supplementation of the mother for two to three months after birth is sometimes advised in order to replenish stores depleted by pregnancy.

B. Vegetarian Menus (without meat, but containing milk products and eggs)

Menus	Calories	Protein (g)	Calcium (mg)	Iron (mg)	Vit. B12 (µg)	Vit. C (mg)
Day 1	1914	86	1857	15	5	168
Day 2	2361	86	1952	14	4	251
Day 3	2331	98	2300	18	9	373
Day 4	2018	96	2336	16	7	184
Day 5	2164	99	2423	15	12	284
Day 6	2076	84	2078	20	4	258
Day 7	2129	95	2067	17	6	144
DAILY AVERAGE	2142[1]	92	2145	16[3]	7[4]	237
UK	2700	73[2]	1200	15	no rec. fig.	60

1. Comments about the caloric values of these vegetarian menus are the same as those made about the meat diet.
2. The protein recommendation of 73 grams per day in a vegetarian diet represents an increase over that of the meat diet and meets the FAO's recommendations in this respect. According to the same source, a vegan diet without meat, milk products, or eggs would require a daily addition of 13 grams of protein; that is, an increase of 21% in relation to the meat diet, to make up for the total absence of food of animal origin.
3. Due to daily consumption of whole-grain cereals and pulses, the average iron values slightly exceed the U.K. recommendation of 15 grams per day. However, it is important to realize that iron, from these sources, is not used as efficiently by the body as the iron from meat or offal. If a vitamin-C rich fruit or vegetable is eaten (orange, broccoli, or other) at meal-time, together with pulses or cereal, iron is absorbed five times more efficiently than if these foods were eaten alone.

4. Adequate amounts of vitamin B12 are found in vegetarian diets since they contain large amounts of milk products and eggs. A vegan diet without meat, poultry, fish, milk products and eggs will not contain enough vitamin B12 and could have serious effects on the mother unless vitamin B12 supplements are added or she adjusts her diet accordingly.

5. Iron needs during lactation are not substantially different from those of non-pregnant women, but continued supplementation for two or three months after birth is sometimes advised in order to replenish stores depleted during pregnancy.

CHAPTER SEVEN

'Other Milks' Before and After Six Months

DURING THE FIRST YEAR of life, breast-milk or a carefully chosen modified milk continues to be the most important baby food and is unequalled in supplying important nutritive elements necessary to the baby's growth. No other food can do as much. During the first six months, milk alone suffices. After this age, solids complete the picture, milk still retaining its principal role.

Many chapters of this book expound upon the benefits of breast-feeding because it is the first and best choice. Unfortunately, at the present time, only a relatively small number of babies (50% in the U.S., 63% in the UK) benefit from it and only for a short period of up to six weeks. By four months only about a quarter of mothers are still breast-feeding in the UK. A vast assortment of milks is thus consumed by babies, and various surveys conducted in Canada and the UK reveal the breakdown of the use of these milks during the first months.

VII-1: *Other Types of Milk Found in a Baby's Diet*

Other types of milk	% of babies drinking at about 6 weeks	% of babies drinking at about 4 months
Skimmed cow's milk with demineralised whey and mixed fats	56	49
Skimmed cow's milk with added carbohydrate and mixed fats	11	13

| Cow's milk with added carbohydrate | 32 | 31 |
| Milk unmodified for babies (cow's, goat's, condensed or evaporated | 1 | 6 |

(*Infant Feeding 1980* OPCS Martin and Monk)

Some babies, breast-fed at birth, also change to other types of milk before the age of six months. In fact a baby might drink three types of milk during the first year of life.

Some milks such as ordinary cow's milk, skimmed or semi-skimmed milk are definitely unsuitable choices to use at birth since they can harm the newborn's organism, while others, such as modified formulas, are recommended. After six months the situation changes, and whole cow's milk can be given without any problem.

In order to provide the baby with the right milk at the right time, let us examine the composition and nutritive value of these various milks. Let it be well understood, however, the final choice should be made in consultation with the doctor. The following modified formulas are recommended for the first six months failing breast-feeding:

- in Canada and in the United States: SMA, Similac, Enfalac, PM 60/40, Enfamil
- in the U.K.: Aptamil, Cow & Gate Premium, Osterfeed, SMA, Gold Cap

Although these milks attempt to imitate breast-milk as much as possible, they cannot, because breast-milk is inimitable. One need only observe the periodic changes made to the composition of these milks and the variations from one milk to the other which follow upon the heels of the most recent discoveries in breast-milk research and recommendations from leading experts in the field.

Nevertheless, on the whole these milks are more suitable to the physiological needs of the newborn than ordinary cow's milk or other available milks; they are the second-best choice after breast-milk.

Modified Milks

1. Composition

Modified milk formulas fall into two categories: those which are highly modified and those which are modified.

The highly modified baby milks contain demineralised whey and some (or all, depending on the manufacturer) of the butterfat, which a baby finds hard to digest, is replaced with vegetable oil and/or beef oleo. Modified baby milks are based on components of cow's milk, consisting of milk, lactose (or a combination of lactose and maltodextrins) and fat, either butterfat and vegetable oil or beef oleo and vegetable oil.

Lactose and also, in the case of some baby milks, maltodextrin, are added because cow's milk contains a lower level of lactose than human breast milk. Lactose is preferable to other types of sugar because, once it is transformed into galactose, it is the only sugar capable of being used for building a baby's brain cells. It also enhances the absorption of calcium.

All modified formulas contain sufficient amounts of iron to meet a normal baby's needs.

1. Nutritive Value

If modified milk formulas are compared to ordinary cow's milk, the nutritive differences which affect the new born's well-being are quickly understood.

VII-2: Table Comparing Humanized Milk Formulas and Cow's Milk

Nutritive Elements	Modified Milk (OsterFeed, Cow & Gate Premium, SMA Gold Cap)	Cow's Milk (whole, homogenized)
Proteins	1.4 g per 100 ml	3.4 g per 100 ml

	• quantity comparable to that found in breast-milk • easier to digest since milk is treated	• quantity exceeding the needs of the newborn • hard to digest
Fats	3.6-3.8 g per 100 ml • vegetable oils + milk fat or vegetable oils + beef fat easier to digest because rich in polyunsaturated fats	3.9 g per 100ml • harder to digest because rich in saturated fats
Lactose	7.0-7.2 g per 100 ml • comparable to amounts found in breast milk	4.6 g per 100 ml • insufficient amounts for human baby
Minerals	calcium 35-44.5 mg per 100 ml phosphorous 27-33 mg per 100 ml potassium 56-60 mg per 100 ml magnesium 4.5-5.3 mg per 100 ml • found in lesser amounts than in cow's milk; comparable to amounts found in breast-milk	calcium 124 mg per 100 ml phosphorous 98 mg per 100 ml potassium 155 mg per 100 ml magnesium 12 mg per 100 ml • greatly exceeds the baby's needs and overloads his immature renal system
Vitamin C	5.5-6.9 mg per 100 ml • amount added is slightly above that present in breast-milk	1.5 mg per 100 ml • amount insufficient to meet needs of human baby
Vitamin D	1.05 μg per 100 ml • amount added exceeds that found in breast milk. Compensates for lack of sun in UK	0.02 μg per 100 ml • amount exceeds that found in breast milk. Compensates for lack of sun in UK

3. Directions for Using Formulas

Modified formulas should be prepared according to the instructions on the package, but keep these points in mind:

- while preparing the milk, use only scrupulously clean utensils which have been rinsed in boiling water
- sugar should never be added, as modified milk contains the proper amount of sugar
- the milk formula is kept in sterilized bottles in the refrigerator until feeding time
- if the product is bought in concentrated liquid form, an equal amount of water is added (tap water must be boiled for twenty minutes, then cooled).
- if the product is bought in powdered form, the correct amount of water and powder is measured out precisely to obtain the mixture suited to the baby's needs
- the ready-to-serve type is available only for use in hospitals.

4. Time of Introduction and Length of Use

For previously mentioned reasons, modified milk formulas are offered right at birth. They can occasionally be used to replace a breast-feeding or become a substitute for breast-feeding as in the case of early weaning.

Apart from breast-milk these are the only milks really suitable to the needs of infants less than six months old. After six months, the baby can gradually be changed from modified formulas to whole cow's milk.

5. Cost

Modified formulas are available in chemists and food stores. Prices vary enormously from one store to the next. It would therefore be wise to visit several stores before buying a large quantity.

Note: bought in powdered form, the cost is half the cost of the liquid form.

Whole Homogenized Cow's Milk

Not recommended before six months

As you can very well see for yourself in Table VII-2, whole homogenized cow's milk is not at all suited to the needs of the newborn human baby.

A baby should not drink this type of milk before six months of age. Whole cow's milk contains hard-to-digest protein and fats as well as too large a quantity of minerals which puts a strain on the baby's immature renal system. Occasionally, it can provoke allergic reactions, intestinal bleeding, and diarrhoea accompanied by fever which can dehydrate the baby.

Note: Evaporated milk has been used, diluted and sweetened, in the past to feed babies. However, although it contains added vitamin D, it is not now recommended for infant feeding because the cow's milk nutrients have not been readjusted to suit the needs of the young child.

No problem after six months

After six months, and once the baby has started eating solids, whole cow's milk can gradually be integrated into his milk diet.

Skimmed and Semi-Skimmed Milk

Not recommended during the first twelve months

Since the beginning of the '70s, it has been noticed that a growing number of babies have been drinking skimmed or semi-skimmed milk since birth or from four to six months onwards under the pretext that this will alleviate problems of atherosclerosis or prevent obesity. However, this practice has recently been proved unwise.

A few researchers eager to discover the effects of this

practice on the child's growth conducted a study on the question. They found that babies given skimmed milk from the age of four months drank larger amounts of milk and ate more solid foods than babies given modified milk in order to obtain the needed energy essential for their growth. In spite of this, the former gained weight less rapidly and lost an important amount of fatty tissue, representing nearly 28% of their reserves over a fifty-six day period as compared to the latter group. This considerable loss of fatty tissue could jeopardize the baby's ability to fight against infections or prolonged illness.

According to the authors, this type of milk, if given too early to the child, instead of preventing obesity seems to trigger a compensatory mechanism making him eat and drink larger quantities of food and milk in an attempt to obtain the desired satiety level. At an older age, faced with a diet richer in calories and fat, the child is unable to limit himself to moderate quantities, since he has acquired the habit of gorging himself to satisfy his appetite, and all this as a result of a too early introduction to skimmed milk.

It is also obvious that a skimmed or semi-skimmed milk diet causes even greater harm in the newborn since it deprives the baby of essential fats normally contained in good quantities in breast-milk or modified milk and in lesser amounts in whole cow's milk.

Semi-skimmed and skimmed milks also provide too much protein and minerals and tax the baby's immature, under-developed renal system. They are 'unbalanced' milks for the newborn as well as for all babies up to one year of age and should be avoided at all costs.

Soya-Based Formulas for Special Cases

It is possible to obtain a variety of other milk formulas based on soya protein (Wysoy, Cow & Gate Formula S). A formula based on chicken meat is sometimes used in hospitals but it is not generally available.

These formulas are used only in special cases, notably when babies are diagnosed allergic to the protein and/or the sugar (lactose) in milk. The baby's physician should be the only one who decides on the use of these formulas.

VII-3: *The Right Milk at the Right Time*

Milk	Introduction Time	Length of Use.
Breast-milk	birth	unlimited, according to the mother's availability
Modified milk formulas	birth	at least to the age of six months
Whole cow's milk	after 6 months and introduction of solids	until age 1 or older (according to family practices)
Semi-skimmed milk	after 1 year	according to the needs and food habits of the family
Skimmed milk	if necessary only after 12 months	according to the needs of the child

CHAPTER EIGHT

Vitamin Supplements Before and After Six Months

W HEN ONE SPEAKS of vitamin or mineral supplements, essentially what is meant is a nutritional complement; the role of this complement is not to help the baby exceed his nutritional needs but rather to provide him with those nutrients which are not present in his daily diet in sufficient amounts. A vitamin or mineral supplement is useful, therefore, to complete the daily diet or to fill nutritional gaps which result when the foods consumed in a day do not provide all the nutritional needs of the baby.

But opinions regarding the use of these supplements are divided, and often even contradictory. This book is not aimed at settling the debate once and for all, as a book can never replace the advice of a medical professional regarding the particular needs of a baby. The following pages present the facts and invite reflection. Before investing in expensive vitamin and mineral supplements, it is advisable to discuss them with your family physician. In any case, a baby who is fed on any of the proprietary baby milk foods should be receiving a sufficient daily intake of both vitamins and minerals. Older children may perhaps need vitamin supplements such as those available at clinics, or Adexolin or Abidec.

The First Six Months

By drawing a parallel between the prescribed supplements, the needs of the baby, and his daily diet, it should be easy to determine if supplements are necessary. Unfortunately, this type of comparison would show only one side of the coin, since the infant has other sources of nutrients. Under ideal conditions, an infant is born with built-in nutrients assimilated during the gestation period. Borne by a well-nourished mother, the baby has had at its disposal nutritional reserves which are difficult to quantify, but are nevertheless real.There is no need to rearrange his daily diet for the sake of a few milligrams above or below his nutritional requirements. Only wide variances should be supplemented and even then there are many exceptions.

To understand the debate better, let us begin by examining the daily contribution of various milks compared to the needs of the baby as estimated in the daily intakes of nutrients recommended by the DHSS. Then we will look at the contribution of the most frequently prescribed supplements and draw the proper conclusions. Each nutritive element is studied separately and calculations are based on two volumes of milk, 800 ml and 1 litre (26 ounces and 31 ounces) in order to take into consideration the increase in the baby's milk consumption from birth to six months.

Vitamin D

Vitamin D is found in sufficient quantities in modified milk. On the other hand, only traces are found in human milk. However, rickets, which is directly related to the lack of vitamin D, is rarely detected in breast-fed babies. Nevertheless, it is wise at this point to recommend a vitamin D supplement for the breast-fed baby.

Since supplements containing only vitamin D are practically nonexistent, a supplement such as Adexolin or Abidec is recommended for breast-fed babies beginning in the second week of life. This is not compulsory as no problems are found in many breast-fed babies who do not take this vitamin, but supplementation seems the prudent thing to do.

VIII-1: Daily Sources of Vitamin D before 6 Months

Infant's requirements 10 μg per day

| Daily Diet | Daily Contribution | | Supplement |
	800 ml (26 oz) as fed	1 litre (31 oz) as fed	Adexolin, Abidec or clinic vitamin drops
Human milk	0.08 μg	0.1 μg	10 drops = 10 μg
OsterFeed Cow & Gate	8.0 μg	10 μg	unnecessary
Premium	8.8 μg	11 μg	unnecessary
SMA Gold Cap	8.4 μg	10.5 μg	unnecessary
Cow's milk (whole) (not recommended)	0.16 μg	0.2 μg	10 drops = 10 μg

Supplement indicated, possibly, for breast fed babies and babies fed on whole cow's milk (not a recommended milk)

Vitamin C

Vitamin C is present in sufficient quantities in all milks recommended for babies. A supplement is therefore not necessary.

On the other hand, a baby fed cow's milk (an unrecommended milk) requires a vitamin C supplement.

Breast-fed babies who are given a vitamin supplement containing three vitamins in order to obtain their quota of vitamin D, could perhaps benefit from vitamin C as it promotes better absorption of the iron found in breast-milk.

VIII-2: Daily Sources of Vitamin C before 6 Months

Infant's requirements 15 mg per day

| Daily Diet | Daily Contribution | | Supplement |
	800 ml (26 oz) as fed	1 litre (31 oz) as fed	Adexolin, Abidec or clinic vitamin drops
Human milk	30.4 mg	38 mg	unnecessary

OsterFeed	55.2 mg	69 mg	unnecessary
Cow & Gate			
Premium	44 mg	55 mg	unnecessary
SMA Gold Cap	46.4 mg	58 mg	unnecessary
Cow's milk (whole) (not recommended)	12 mg	15 mg	unnecessary

Supplement unnecessary to all milks, but forms component of all vitamin drops and brings the vitamin C content of cow's milk up to the level of that found in modified milks.

Vitamin A

The baby's vitamin A requirements are satisfactorily met by his milk diet regardless of the type of milk used (Table VIII-3). The supplement simply provides a nonessential additional amount which, if administered in the proper dosage, does not harm the baby. We could ask ourselves why this vitamin continues to be present in these supplements when it rarely corresponds to a real deficiency in the baby's diet.

VIII-3: Daily Sources of Vitamin A before 6 Months

Infant's requirements 450 μg per day

| Daily Diet | Daily Contribution | | Supplement |
	800 ml (26 oz) as fed	1 litre (31 oz) as fed	Adexolin, Abidec or clinic vitamin drops
Human milk	480 μg	600 μg	unnecessary
OsterFeed	800 μg	1,000 μg	unnecessary
Cow & Gate			
Premium	640 μg	800 μg	unnecessary
SMA Gold Cap	632 μg	790 μg	unnecessary

| Cow's milk (whole) (not recommended) | 320 μg | 400 μg | 10 drops = 450 μg |

Supplement unnecessary to all milks, except cow's milk (not a recommended milk) to which the addition of 10 ACD vitamin drops per day brings the vitamin A content up to the level of that found in modified milks.

B Vitamins

Some supplements (eg. Abidec) contain vitamins from the B-complex (thiamin, riboflavin, niacin and vitamin B6) as well as vitamins A, D, and C. These vitamins are rarely necessary because breast-milk, modified milk, or whole concentrated milk, diluted and sweetened, contain sufficient amounts of these vitamins.

In a few cases, an additional quantity of B vitamins could be required for the baby who drinks soya-based milk because of milk allergies. In such cases, the family doctor is your best guide.

Fluoride

Despite its rather controversial reputation, fluoride is a particularly important nutrient during the formative years. It has a marked effect on tooth formation, and many painful moments spent in the dentist's chair are avoided because fluoride helps form tooth enamel which is more resistant to various decay-producing agents. It has been found that regular drinking of fluoridated water helps reduce tooth decay by as much as 50% to 60%.

Since natural fluoride in food is quite limited, water fluoridation remains the best method of providing this nutrient to the population. The latest figures from the Department of the Environment show that 10% of the population in the UK now receives fluoride in the public water supply. This is 5.3 million people. Birmingham became the first major city to fluoridate its water supply in 1964 and a survey published in 1979 showed that children there aged between four and five years suffered 54% less decayed, missing and filled teeth than those of the same age group living in Salford where water is not fluoridated. Fluoridation of the water in Birmingham halved the cost of treatment needed for caries in children's teeth.

Until such time as all drinking water is fluoridated, babies in unfluoridated regions should receive a fluoride supplement after six months. Fluoride is effective mainly at teething time, and the supplement appears to be unnecessary and unbeneficial before a baby is six months old. Since it is often prescribed along with other vitamins at two weeks of age, a baby could feasibly take fluoride supplements from the second week following birth without danger.

A supplement such as En-de-Kay contains fluoride exclusively, and a daily dose of seven drops (0.25 mg) satisfies a baby's needs before or after six months in an unfluoridated area.'

Iron

Iron is part of the nutritional package received at birth. As all packages differ, this one, stored up during the last three months of pregnancy, is not equal in all newborn babies. A normal-weight baby born at term, has good iron reserves for the next four months. A premature baby born at seven or eight months has generally exhausted all his iron reserves in two months. Babies cannot all be treated in the same way.

A baby also receives iron from the milk he drinks:

- Breast-milk contains little iron but the iron it has is absorbed five times more efficiently than that in ordinary cow's milk. For this reason, breast-milk satisfies the baby's iron requirements entirely for at least six months without adding solid foods to his diet.
- Modified formula, (OsterFeed, Cow & Gate Premium,

SMA Gold Cap) provides sufficient iron for a normal weight infant born at term for up to twelve months of age.

As a general rule:

1. A normal-weight baby fed exclusively breast-milk for six months, without solids being added, does not need iron supplements until six months of age.

2. A normal-weight baby, fed modified formula (Oster-Feed, Cow & Gate Premium, SMA Gold Cap) does not need additional iron.

3. A baby who is weaned on to cow's milk at six months or so may need an iron supplement if he is not eating baby cereals, which have iron added in sufficient quantities to meet his needs. Iron in too large quantities is toxic and should never be given unless under medical advice.

VIII-4: *Supplement Requirements for the Normal-Weight Baby, Born at Term, During the First 6 Months*

Nutritive Element	Maternal Milk	Modified Milk (Cow & Gate Premium OsterFeed, SMA Gold Cap)	Concentrated (Whole Milk)
Vitamin D	supplement 'prudent' at two weeks 10 µg/day	unnecessary	unnecessary
Vitamin C	unnecessary	unnecessary	unnecessary
Vitamin A	unnecessary	unnecessary	unnecessary
Fluoride	unnecessary	unnecessary	unnecessary
Iron	unnecessary	unnecessary	supplement necessary after 4 months (5-10 mg/day or iron-enriched baby cereals)

There is no general rule for underweight or premature babies. Your doctor should be consulted.

Six to Eighteen Months

A mother who gradually adds iron-enriched baby cereals, vegetables, poultry, fish or meat (pulses if vegetarian), and fruit to the baby's diet, sees that he receives all the required nutrients, provided a good supply of milk continues to be consumed. Such babies do not need vitamin or mineral supplements except fluoride if the water authority where the baby lives does not add it to the drinking water. In this case 0.25 mg of fluoride, given in the form of En-De-Kay drops, represents the daily dose recommended up to age two.

Should a baby constantly refuse to eat one or more important food groups, a supplement should be added to his diet:

- The child who drinks only a small amount of milk or does not eat dairy products needs a supplement of calcium, vitamin D, and B vitamins
- the vegan child who does not eat eggs, milk, milk products, meat, poultry, or fish needs a vitamin D plus calcium and B12 supplement
- the child who constantly refuses to eat any fruit or vegetables benefits by taking vitamin A, C and D supplements (see Chapter Eleven for role and daily requirements of these vitamins from birth to six years).

CHAPTER NINE

Solid Foods: Slowly but Surely

EARLY IN THIS century the infant ate no solid food before the age of one. This was the era of the fat, 'milk-fed' baby. According to an extensive survey conducted in 1976, 40% of babies were eating cereals by the age of two weeks, and one out of every two babies was receiving meat by three and a half months. This was the era of the 'force-fed' baby.

This premature introduction to solid foods reflects the type of advice once given by certain doctors since very few mothers will on their own alter their baby's diet. However, in recent years research has shown that babies are not really ready to take solid food before the age of three or four months. Accordingly health visitors, doctors and baby food manufacturers themselves recommend the gradual introduction of solid food, starting with cereals, from the age of three to four months. If a baby is introduced too early to solid foods he won't be able to take so much milk, he will lose valuable sucking time and he may become dehydrated. A recent and extensive study of the eating habits of babies in the UK (*Martin and Monk Infant Feeding 1980*) shows that the majority of babies surveyed are not being fed solids until they reach three months of age. This is a good step in the right direction.

Infant nutrition experts and officials from various government bodies, are unanimous in saying that there are no advantages to be gained by introducing solids to babies before the age of four to six months.

Physiological, Nutritive and Anti-Allergenic Reasons for Introducing Solids after Four to Six Months of Age

The opinions and advice given by health professionals today is fairly consistent although some may vary by a few weeks, more or less, but the underlying message remains the same: 'Before four to six months, a breast-fed baby receiving a vitamin D supplement, or a baby on a humanized milk formula, receives all the nourishment he needs.'

This recommendation is based on arguments which are difficult to refute.

A. Solids have no effect on the length of the baby's sleep periods

Controlled scientific observations demonstrate that no relationship exists between the introduction of solid foods and the number of hours of nocturnal sleep a baby will have under four months of age. Many babies fed milk exclusively sleep all night long before four months. Prolonged sleep represents a baby's neurological development and has nothing to do with his eating habits.

B. Before a certain age, a baby is not physically ready to swallow solids

Before three months of age, a baby does not salivate very much, and his tongue is not able to push the food towards the back of his mouth. His suction reflex is well developed but his ingurgitation reflex is not; he has great trouble swallowing foods of a solid consistency. The neuromuscular coordination which enables him to eat solid foods adequately is reached around sixteen to eighteen weeks.

C. The newborn's digestive system is underdeveloped

At birth a baby is not equipped with all the digestive apparatus essential for the digestion of many foods. A full-term baby has only a fraction of the digestive enzymes or substances normally present in the six-month or two-year-old child. Before he has reached the age of three or four months, he is not ready to digest cereals or other starches and, before four to six months, he absorbs only part of the fats. A baby who eats solids too early only partially assimilates them and does so with great difficulty; what remains is found in his stools.

D. A baby's renal system is immature

The newborn infant is not really completely developed; his renal system is incomplete and very vulnerable to food excesses. Some foods, if given too early (meat, egg yolk), place a burden on the kidneys and may cause serious problems in more fragile babies or in babies drinking ordinary cow's milk during the first few months of life.

E. The younger the baby the higher the risks of allergic reactions

The immune defence system which protects the baby against hostile invaders is still incomplete in the four-to-eight-week-old baby. The addition of solid food at this time could provoke an allergic reaction. The production of antibodies increases gradually during the first year, peaking at seven months. A slow and gradual introduction of solids after four to six months reduces the risks of allergic reactions particularly in babies whose families have a history of allergies.

F. A full-term baby does not require iron until four to six months

A full-term breast-fed baby given exclusively breast-milk does not require iron until he reaches the age of six months, while a baby fed milk which has not been iron-enriched uses up iron reserves by the time he is four months old.

Baby cereals given between four to six months help meet increased dietary iron needs. Before that their contribution is superfluous.

G. Early introduction of solid foods does not increase the nutritive value of the diet

In spite of his immature digestive, renal, and immunological development, the young baby does possess a satiety mechanism. For this reason when he is fed solid foods at too early an age, he automatically reduces his milk consumption.

In order to quantify this phenomenon properly, comparative studies have been carried out on the nutritive values of the diet of infants fed exclusively on milk and of the diet of those fed on milk and solids. The studies found that up to the age of three months the two diets were equal from the nutritional standpoint. The milk and solid diet is not superior because the baby is satisfied more quickly and drinks less milk. Solids replace milk, instead of complementing the milk, and are often (as in the case of cereals, fruits, and vegetables) less useful to the baby.

For the same number of calories, solids provide less of the important nutritive elements and may decrease the nutritive value of the entire diet of the baby.

H. The slow introduction of solids respects a baby's appetite

Around five or six months, a baby can easily sit up with support and has better neuromuscular control of his head and neck. He can reveal his hunger by moving his head forward and indicate his satiety by moving it back. Before a baby can do these movements or give these distinct messages, the feeding of solids is tantamount to force-feeding.

It is only possible to respect a baby's appetite, to foster good nutritive habits and prevent overeating, when he can clearly indicate his hunger and his satisfaction. This final point is of prime importance to this author, and is a stepping-stone in forming good eating habits.

The Ideal Time for Introducing Solids

Between four to six months of age, a baby not only is able to swallow and digest a certain number of foods, but he also gradually acquires the capacity to chew solid food. He is also ready to experience new foods as far as texture and flavour are concerned. With half of his year behind him, the six-month-old baby is able to chew solid foods regardless of the fact the he has few teeth, if any.

If the introduction of solids is delayed until nine or ten months, the value of this particularly sensitive and positive period could be lost. The older baby resists being fed foods of thicker consistency, and having a change in his diet. It is more difficult for him to accept ordinary foods and he could demand strained baby food for a very long time.

Although everyone may agree on the ideal time for the introduction of solids, there is no universally perfect time for all babies. Each baby is different and should be treated as such. Few guidelines are available which can determine the precise and ideal time for a given baby. A baby's growth and general behaviour are the best indicators to parents and to the family doctor.

- *The total amount of milk consumed during the day is not an absolute criteria.* Milk volume often varies from one baby to the next. A breast-fed baby drinks an unknown quantity of milk; a small baby at birth drinks less milk than a bigger one; the four-or five-month-old baby can easily drink about forty ounces of milk per day. In fact, no fixed rule exists which applies to all.
- *The number of feedings per day can sometimes be a poor indicator.* Up to four or five months of age, a baby drinks at least four times a day. If the number of feedings is reduced to three too quickly, a baby will have trouble drinking enough milk at each feeding. In such a situation, a baby demonstrating his hunger requires an additional milk feeding, and not solids.

- *Crying does not always indicate hunger.* Proper interpretation of the cries of a baby requires considerable parental intuition and sensitivity, and it is sometimes easier to attribute crying to hunger than to some other cause. By using the 'milk or food' method as a last recourse, after eliminating other common sources of discomfort (dirty nappies, uncomfortable positon, need for music and light, thirst), the various needs of the child are better respected and overfeeding is avoided.

Baby Cereals: A Necessity

The argument for or against commercially prepared baby foods has somewhat tarnished the reputation of baby cereals. They have been accused of not meeting the nutritional needs of the infant and of containing sugar. However, if their nutritive contribution of protein, B vitamins and minerals is considered, these accusations appear unfounded!

Easily eaten and digested because they are precooked and reduced to a fine powder, these cereals are specially prepared to meet the needs of babies and to supply an important quantity of iron at a time when a baby's reserves are almost exhausted. These cereals are even preferable to oatmeal and other whole-grain cereals since they are enriched with a type of iron, particularly well suited to a baby's digestive system, to a level based on the absorptive capacity of the baby's digestive system.

Reports from a recent survey of the food and nutrient intake of over 400 infants during their first eighteen months of life indicate that the iron intake of these infants was low from twelve months onwards. Lack of adequate iron was attributed to early termination of iron-fortified infant cereals; many infants were eating adult-type cereals that were fortified with iron at a much lower level than the infant cereals.

Since they are nutritious and difficult to replace with ordinary cereals, it is sometimes recommended that they be included in a baby's diet up to eighteen months of age.

It is true that while cereals containing sugar are still on the market, they are fewer and fewer in numbers. Well-informed consumers can easily avoid buying sweetened cereals by reading the labels. Farley, for example, now produces a low sugar rusk. This goes also for gluten, milk and fructose content, all of which can be avoided in the Robinson's cereal range.

IX-1: *A Practical Guide to the Introduction of Cereals*

Time of introduction: between four and six months

Contribution:
- baby's iron reserves are nearly exhausted; cereals contribute good amounts of iron
- cereals provide iron, B vitamins, protein and additional needed calories

Procedure:
- start with the cereals less likely to produce an allergic reaction (rice, barley, soya)
- begin with one teaspoon of cereal mixed with formula milk or breast-milk
- always spoon-feed in order to provide baby with exercise for the mouth muscles
- never add sugar
- serve the same cereal four or five days consecutively before introducing a new one
- gradually increase the amount to a maximum of eight tablespoons daily by the end of the first year
- cereals with fruit added are not recommended

Vegetables: A Way of Adding Colour to the Diet

Vegetables should be added to the baby's diet one month after starting cereals. They add colour, texture, and flavour and are more easily accepted if offered before fruit. They are also low in calories and add vitamins and food fibre to the newborn's diet.

Carrots are quite popular and are a good way to get things started. They should be followed by a variety of green, yellow, or white vegetables: green beans, courgettes, green peas, broccoli, marrow, swede, cauliflower and celery.

Potatoes come last, around seven months, to complement the other vegetables and not to replace them.

IX-2: *A Practical Guide to the Introduction of Vegetables*

Time of introduction: one month after the introduction of cereals

Contribution:
- provide vitamins, minerals, and food fibre
- develop baby's taste buds

Procedure:
- introduce one vegetable at a time: wait four or five days before offering another one
- give each vegetable separately before offering a mixture of vegetables
- always give cooked vegetables
- use homemade purees or commercial baby food
- never add salt, sugar or fat
- gradually increase the amount from 1 teaspoon to a maximum of 10 tablespoons towards the end of the first year
- always spoon-feed

Fruit for Dessert

Fruit stimulates a baby's taste buds and is easily integrated into his diet! Fruits supply vitamins, minerals, food fibre, and a permissible type of sugar. Apples, pears, bananas, peaches and apricots form an interesting variety. Unsweetened fruit juice also provides vitamins and minerals and it tastes good.

IX-3: A Practical Guide to the Introduction of Fruit

Time of introduction: three or four weeks after the introduction of vegetables

Contribution:
- vitamins, minerals, and food fibre
- flavour and permissible sugar

Procedure:
- offer each fruit separately before blending a mixture of fruit or fruit purees
- use homemade purees or commercial baby food
- offer cooked fruit except for ripe bananas which can simply be mashed with a fork
- small fruits such as strawberries, raspberries, gooseberries, and grapes contain small seeds which may present some problems and should be avoided until the age of eighteen to twenty-four months
- never add sugar
- avoid fruit desserts
- to quench a baby's thirst, water is preferable to repeated use of fruit juice
- 2 oz. of orange juice daily will meet all vitamin C needs

Meat, Poultry, Fish or Substitutes Complete the Menu

Providing important sources of protein, this food group is the last to be added to a baby's menu. Since the nutrients in meats and meat substitutes are more concentrated than in cereals, vegetables and fruit, they are better tolerated by the baby who is over six months of age.

Several fish, such as cod, haddock, sole, plaice and whiting, contain very little fat, have a delicate flavour, and provide protein of excellent quality.

Chicken liver is economical and nutritious, and can occasionally replace meat, providing an important amount of iron.

Cooked and mashed pulses or tofu (cheese made from the soya bean) contain good amounts of vegetable protein and can ensure normal growth for a vegetarian baby when adequately complemented in the diet.

One daily meat, poultry, or fish portion meets the nutritional needs of a baby.

IX-4: *A Practical Guide to the Introduction of Meat or Meat Substitutes*

Time of introduction: two to three weeks after the integration of fruit; this enables incorporation of only one food group at a time.

Contribution:
- excellent source of protein
- meat, liver, and pulses rich in iron
- poultry and fish contain less fat than meat

Procedure:
- start with white meat (chicken, turkey) or fish
- use homemade purees or commercial baby food (pureed meat of one type only)
- at the start, do not mix with vegetables in order to encourage the distinguishing of different flavours
- never add salt
- gradually increase from a small amount to a maximum of 6 tablespoons daily towards the end of the first year
- the vegetarian baby can substitute cottage cheese, tofu, or cooked, pureed pulses for meat
- serve this food group preferably at the noon meal

Other Foods

Egg Yolk

Hardened and mashed in small quantities into pureed vegetables or meat, egg yolk is introduced into a baby's diet at the same time as meat or meat substitutes. It supplies protein, vitamins and minerals, but is no longer considered a good source of iron.

One teaspoon (5 ml) per day is recommended at the beginning, preferably given at the noon meal, and it is gradually increased to a maximum of three egg yolks per weeks around twelve months of age. This food is not essential and can be eliminated from the diet in a high risk family; that is, a family with a history of high blood cholesterol levels.

Whole Egg

Since egg white causes more allergies than the yolk, the whole egg is introduced towards the end of the first year of life, when the baby's antibody system is better developed.

After one year, a poached or hard-boiled egg can be served four times a week without any problems. As it is easily digested, it can be eaten at night surrounded by colourful vegetables. Once the whole egg has been integrated into the baby's diet there is no longer any need to serve egg yolk alone.

Yogurt

When the baby is eating a wide variety of food (cereals, vegetables, fruit, meat, and meat substitutes), yogurt can be added. Ideally plain yogurt is offered first, either homemade or commercially prepared, without the addition of sugar or fruit. (Homemade yogurt is less sour than the commercial preparation and more easily accepted.)

When a baby is familiar with the flavour of plain yogurt and his appetite is increasing, pieces of mashed fruit can be added (ripe bananas, unsweetened apple sauce, poached pears, etc.).

Yogurt in baby-food jars is now available. This is undeniably less sweet than ordinary fruit yogurts but does not offer all the benefits of the lactic culture since it is sterilized.

Honey: not before one year

Since 1975, cases of infantile botulism have occasionally been reported in the United States and botulism has accounted for several unexpected baby deaths. Analysis of hundreds of foods either likely to have been, or in fact, actually consumed by the babies, revealed that only honey contained botulism spores and that these spores could cause sudden death in very young children.

In the U.K., where only one case of infant botulism has been reported since 1978, the Public Health Authority recommends that babies younger than eighteen months should not be given honey, especially imported honey. Beyond that age, the body can fight the action of the spores, if present, because the gut contains the normal, adult, bacteria balance.

Fruit Juices

When fruit is introduced, fruit juices can be started as well. Apple juice is the best first choice since it does not cause any allergic reactions. Orange juice can be given next.

Fruit juices are served at room temperature. They are never boiled as heating destroys the vitamin C content, and are served in a small tumbler with a drinking spout rather than in a bottle. Two ounces of juice suffice in meeting vitamin C requirements.

Fruit-flavour crystals, sold in package form, do not contain one iota of fruit and should be avoided even if vitamin C is added.

Processed Meats

Bacon, salted and pressed meats, pâtés and smoked sausages, contain a large amount of salt and fat; they are foods not recommended in a baby's diet, particularly during the first twelve months.

Food mashed with a fork

About six months of age, a baby is better able to chew and easily accepts food of a coarser consistency. Food which has been blended is very often replaced by food which is mashed with a fork. From nine to eighteen months of age (see Chapter Twelve), the child usually goes through a transition period during which his diet changes to one which closely resembles that of the family diet, both in variety and texture, with only a few notable exceptions.

Teething Foods

During the long teething period which lasts between four and twenty-four months, certain foods seem to soothe the baby and help him bite and relieve his tender gums. Melba toast and rusks can be useful. However, raw vegetables such as carrots and celery sticks should not be given until the baby is twelve months old. If they are swallowed whole or only partially chewed, they could choke the child.

Unrequired Foods

Packet custards, cakes, sweet biscuits, sweets, chocolates, and other such desserts should not be part of the baby's diet. These treats add calories, develop a baby's sweet tooth, and will lower the nutritive value of the diet by interfering with a baby's appetite and by replacing more important foods.

The Up-To-Date Report on Commercial Baby Food

A favourite target of nutritionists and well-informed consumers, commercial baby food manufacturers have turned over a new leaf in the U.K. and the United States.

The major British producers of baby foods now eliminate the use of salt in all baby food and have reduced the amount of sugar in all fruit and dessert baby foods.

Some types of fruit in jars, currently available in supermarkets, do not have one gram of sugar added. For example: apple sauce for babies and juniors and pear puree for babies and juniors. Check the labels to see if sugar is added or not. Low sugar rusks are also available from Farley and Cow & Gate.

The baby-food industry has to be commended in view of these vast improvements which encourage good nutritional habits for babies. Some general information about the content of these baby food jars remains to be added.

Starch content in baby food

Commercial baby food contains a certain amount of either tapioca, corn starch, barley, or rice flour for proper consistency and to prevent separation of ingredients. These starches do not affect in any way the nutritional value of these products, and are not challenged by nutritional experts, as long as quantities are limited.

Other starches, such as rice and noodles, are part of vegetable and meat preparations. These meals compare favourably with homemade recipes and should not be down-graded if well assimilated into a diet.

Few food additives in these jars

Commercial baby food contains no artificial food colours or flavours. No preservatives are required since these preparations are heated and hermetically sealed in their jars.

Other ingredients in commercial baby food

In order to fully understand baby food labels, a brief explanation about certain terms would be useful.

Reduced iron or electrolytic iron:

- All baby cereals are now enriched with 'reduced' iron, also called 'electrolytic' iron. These iron particles are more easily absorbed by a baby's digestive system than the other type of iron previously used. For this reason, and because the iron content of regular whole-grain cereals destined for the general population is lower, baby cereals are, by far, the best choice for babies.

Dicalcium phosphate:

- For several years now, manufacturers have been adding calcium and phosphorous in the form of dicalcium phosphate, to baby cereals in order to ensure the proper development of bones and teeth, thus complementing the role of milk. This type of enrichment is currently the object of considerable debate.

Citric acid:

- An acid found in fruit which reduces heating time and prevents oxidation in many baby food desserts and fruit purees.

Ascorbic acid:

- A natural emulsifying agent which is added to a number of baby cereals currently available in the UK and which facilitates the manufacturing process and improves the texture.

Hydrogenated vegetable oil:

- An oil which is added to some baby cereals and desserts in order to improve the texture and the taste.

Bacterial culture:

- A lactic bacteria culture is essential in the manufacture of all yogurts. It is found in baby-food yogurts, but because they are sterilized, the action of these cultures is greatly reduced.

The presence of these food additives is controlled and limited in the UK by the Food and Drugs Act.

Nutritive contents of baby food jars

When a table of food composition for commercial baby foods is consulted, it is evident that the quantity of protein, vitamins, and minerals compares favourably with that of the original food used. Well-chosen commercial baby food is nutritious.

During the first few months during which a baby requires smooth food purees, a mother can choose:

- plain vegetables and not creamed or with butter added
- fruit or fruit mixtures, not desserts, custards or fruit supremes
- when meat is first introduced, pureed meats are given; later, dinners may be given
- vegetable and meat dinners can occasionally be served at night, when a lighter meal is preferred.

Baby food costs

If you compare the cost of commercial baby food with that of homemade purees you will find that commercial food costs about twice as much. This difference, which has been verified more than once, applies equally to fruit, vegetables and meat. The calculation is based on the average cost for a variety of fruit and vegetables, fresh or frozen, as well as meats, poultry and fish which could be used in preparing homemade purees.

The cost of a blender or a food processor may seem expensive initially, but when the cost is spread over several years of use, it is quite minimal.

Preparation time is a factor to be considered, but how many mothers calculate the amount of time spent in preparing food? Preparing baby foods can also be done at the same time as other food preparations, and passes almost unnoticed when calculated as part of the total time spent in the kitchen.

CHAPTER TEN

Homemade Baby Food –
A New Challenge

A SURVEY CONDUCTED in Canada in November, 1978 showed that one out of five mothers served only homemade baby food to her child, while 60% of all mothers surveyed regularly prepared some of their own baby foods while supplementing their babies' diets with commercial baby foods. In the UK a survey showed that 3% of mothers started their babies on solids with homemade food exclusively.

Vegetables and fruits are the foods which are most often pureed, followed by poultry, meat, liver and fish. The baby's diet should be varied and the foods well prepared; however, there are a few cases where the food is too highly salted and sweetened. A few years ago, homemade baby foods were analyzed and were often found to contain more salt than commercial baby foods.

If homemade baby food is to contain all of the ingredients essential to health we must be careful not to repeat the past errors of the baby-food producers. It is especially important to watch:

Salt content

1. use only fresh vegetables or salt-free frozen vegetables
2. never use canned vegetable liquid
3. never add salt to baby food either during or after cooking

Sugar content

1. preferably use fresh fruit or unsweetened canned or frozen fruit

2. always discard the sweetened juice from canned fruit and rinse the fruit carefully before placing in the blender
3. avoid the use of sugar, honey or syrup in fruit purees

The Advantages of Homemade Baby Food

As seen in the previous chapter, commercial baby food has significant nutritive value. The systematic elimination of salt and the gradual reduction of sugar from these baby foods has made them quite acceptable from a nutritional standpoint, but one can save a considerable amount of money by preparing homemade baby food. On the basis of the purchasing cost of ingredients only, homemade baby food costs 50% less than commercially prepared foods.

When flavour and variety are considered, homemade baby foods permit the use of a wide variety of vegetables and fish, and allow the use of seasonal foods which are always tasty and full of vitamins.

If nutritive value is considered, homemade baby food, carefully prepared and adequately refrigerated or frozen, retains a large percentage of the original nutrients found in natural food. Homemade preparations are apparently more concentrated since starch is not added. Therefore, portion sizes should be smaller.

An Easy Challenge

The decision to prepare one's own baby food often reflects a liking for cooking in general as well as a personal conviction that it is the best for the baby.

The suggested method of preparation requires a minimum of time and culinary techniques. It is suggested that small amounts of foods be regularly frozen in individual portions to allow the accumulation of small reserves of food and thereby eliminate last-minute preparations.

The purchase of a blender or a food processor is not essential but they make the task easier. In fact, as the baby needs finely pureed foods for only a limited time, a food mill can also be used.

The Rules of the Game

In order to compete with the hygienic and nutritional qualities of commercially prepared baby food, certain general guidelines should be observed. These may seem exhaustive at first glance but careful reading is needed before going on to the recipe stage.

1. Choose high-quality ingredients

The final quality of pureed foods greatly depends on the quality of the ingredients initially chosen. This, of course, applies to all food preparations but is especially important in the preparation of baby food.

Fresh fruit and vegetables that are ripe, and are the proper colour and firmness will always be the best choice. Fruit canned in heavy sweet syrup and canned vegetables with a lot of salt are not recommended for baby-food purees. When fresh fruit and vegetables are not available, or are too expensive, unsweetened and unsalted frozen fruit and vegetables with no sauce or flavouring, or fruit canned in its own juice, are suitable alternatives.

Meat, poultry, and fish must also be chosen according to strict rules regarding freshness and quality. Frozen fish is a valid choice, but canned fish generally contains too much salt for a baby under twelve months of age.

2. Vary the menu

A baby eating a consistent diet of carrots and potatoes, six or seven days a week, is not eating a varied diet. The essential nutrients favourable to growth and health are only found in a variety of food. New foods and new flavours are easily accepted by a baby, and since this is a period of large appetites and of few food whims, you must take advantage of this.

You can alternate green and yellow vegetables on the menu and gradually add potatoes as the baby's appetite increases. Either lean meat, poultry or fish should be selected to provide variety at the main daily meal. The need to offer a variety of food to the baby does not mean an increase in the preparation time at each meal. Thanks to the freezer, you can prepare food when you feel like it, or when time permits, and freeze it in individual portions for future meals.

3. Follow a few hygienic rules

In order to eliminate the possibility of food contamination and to protect the baby from infections, certain simple rules should be observed:

- wash hands well before handling any food which will be used to prepare homemade baby food
- use utensils and containers that have been impeccably cleaned
- cover the food well once cooked and refrigerate immediately; do not allow to stand at room temperature
- when baby food is prepared in small quantities and unfrozen, do not keep the food more than three days in the refrigerator
- do not refreeze a thawed puree.

4. Assemble the necessary utensils

Since solids or homemade purees are introduced only between four and six months of age, very smooth purees or purees without lumps need only be prepared for a few months. From six to eight months, a baby's chewing ability enables him to easily eat food mashed by a fork. A blender or food processor will make the job much easier. However, if you do not wish to invest in such expensive appliances, an inexpensive manual food mill can also be used.

The following utensils will also be needed: containers, measuring cups and measuring spoons, individual ice-cube containers, freezer bags with ties (capacity: 1 pint, or 2 pints, depending on the quantities to be prepared), small aluminium plates, labels.

5. Cook the food rapidly

Cooking makes digestion easier. In addition, when done properly, it retains the highest percentage of nutrients. Vegetables should be either steamed or cooked in a small amount of boiling water in order to minimize vitamin losses. Rapid-cooking periods are preferable to prolonged cooking periods. Tender yet firm vegetables contain more vitamins than limp and discoloured vegetables. Obviously, frozen vegetables should not be thawed before cooking, and the cooking period must be very short.

It is recommended that poultry, meat or fish be cooked in a certain amount of liquid. Fresh fruit, on the other hand, is peeled and poached in a small amount of unsweetened water or fruit juice, except for ripe bananas which can simply be mashed with a fork or pureed in the blender.

Cooking water should be used as much as possible in preparing purees because quite a few of the nutrients present in vegetables, meat or fruit remain in water after cooking.

6. Puree rapidly

Cooked food which has been cooled slightly is placed into the blender. The consistency of the puree will vary depending on a baby's age, but overblending should be avoided in order to minimize the loss of nutrients. For a more liquid puree, more cooking water is added and the mixture is blended again. As a general rule, if the food takes too long to liquify, the amount of liquid may be insufficient or the pieces of food could be too large or too numerous. One and a half to two cups of food can be pureed at one time. However, in the cases of poultry or meat, only one cup of food should be used. Additional quantities hamper the operation of the blender and the final quality of the product is affected.

7. Pour into containers and cool

Once the puree is finished, it is poured into ice-cube containers. Each cube contains about two ounces of food. The puree is then cooled in the refrigerator before freezing.

8. Freeze

The cooled ice-cube containers are then covered with a sheet of waxed paper and placed in the coldest part of the freezer, far from the door. Eight to twelve hours are needed for freezing to take place. Purees can be kept in the freezer for varying lengths of time, depending on the ingredients. The following table shows the maximum time for which various homemade purees may be kept frozen at 0 °F (-18 °C).

X-1: Freezer Storage Time for Homemade Purees

Food	Freezing Period
vegetables	6 to 8 months
fruits	6 to 8 momths
fruits with tapioca	6 weeks
meat and poultry, cooked	10 weeks
(chicken, veal, beef, turkey)	
fish, cooked	10 weeks
vegetable and meat meal	10 weeks
purees containing milk	4 to 6 weeks

9. Place frozen purees in plastic bags

Once the purees are frozen, remove the ice-cube trays from the freezer and empty the individually frozen purees into small polythene bags, one type of food per bag. The bag is then sealed after withdrawing the air with a straw, and is properly labelled as to the type of food as well as the preparation date. The bags are then returned to the freezer.

10. Take out one or two cubes from the bag and warm in a double boiler

At mealtime, the desired number of cubes is removed from the freezer bags. Vegetables, meat, and poultry are then warmed in a double boiler. Fruit requires less thawing time.

NOTE: If last-minute preparation involving a small quantity of food is desired, steps one to six are followed. The puree stored in a closed container can be kept in the refrigerator three days without any problems.

It is strongly recommended that vegetables, fruit and meat be given plain at the start. Once the baby has tasted the individual flavours, mixtures, such as apples and pears, can be offered.

11. Heating baby foods in the microwave

Many homemade as well as commercial foods may be heated in the microwave oven. Here are some important tips to follow:

– Baby foods that contain substantial amounts of meat should not be heated in microwave ovens. Plain meats, poultry, high meat dinners, egg yolks and meat sticks should be warmed by conventional methods. Microwave heating of these foods results in uneven heating that could cause the jar to explode. Droplets of water in the food heat faster by microwaves than the dense protein and fat particles. The water turns to steam in small pockets. Shaking the jar or dish when removing from the microwave or just stirring the food with a spoon could lead to a hot splatter or scald.

– To heat a food item, put it either in a dish or, if in a baby jar, place the *opened* jar on a plate, and insert into the oven. Be sure to remove any caps and leave them outside the oven. Start the oven on the warm setting, or at the lowest level of heat, and test frequently until the food reaches feeding temperature. You may want to record the time and temperature for future reference. Avoid over-heating.

– Consult the manufacturer's instruction booklet or your

dealer before putting baby food in the microwave.
– Reusable baby bottles containing milk may be warmed in the microwave; observe the same precautions as with baby foods listed above. Overheating causes milk to boil over the bottle rim. Bottles should not have the caps or teats on when being warmed. Disposable baby bottles (bags) should not be microwave heated.

RECIPES ('Cup' refers to American measuring cup: 1 cup = $\frac{1}{2}$ pint)

Puree of Carrots

Ingredients
2 lb. (1 kg) fresh carrots
Water

Preparation
1. Peel carrots and cut into 1 inch (2.5 cm) pieces. Place them into a small amount of boiling water. Cover and simmer 20 to 30 minutes or until tender.
2. Place $\frac{3}{4}$ lb of the carrots and ⅓ cup (85 ml) of fresh water into the blender. Puree. Repeat with the remaining carrots. Pour into ice-cube trays and freeze.

Yield
2 ice-cube trays

Storage Life
6 to 8 months

Comments
Fresh carrots are always a better buy than the frozen or canned variety; they can be cooked in a pressure cooker or steamed before they are pureed. Carrots represent an excellent choice because babies are usually fond of them and they also provide an excellent source of vitamin A.

NOTE: Despite certain warnings about the use of homemade carrot purees, this vegetable does not present any problems if carefully prepared with fresh water, refrigerated, and then frozen rapidly, especially when it is offered to a baby who is older than four months.

Puree of Green Beans

Ingredients
1 ½ lb. (700g) fresh and tender green beans
1 teaspoon (5g) minced onion (optional)
Water

Preparation
1. Wash the beans; top and tail them and cut into thirds. Place beans and onions into a small amount of boiling water. Cover and simmer for 20 to 25 minutes or until beans are tender but still bright green. Remove from heat and cool slightly.
2. Place half of the cooked beans and ⅓ cup (85 ml) of the cooking water into the blender. Puree. Repeat with remaining beans.
3. Pour into ice-cube trays and freeze.

Yield
2 ice-cube trays

Storage life
6 to 8 months

Comments
To make good puree, green beans must be young and tender. Frozen green beans may also be used in this recipe.

NOTE: Start with plain beans without the onion at first, then proceed to a combination of flavours later on.

Puree of Parsnips

1½ lb. (700 g) parsnips
(3 medium parsnips)
Water

Preparation
1. Peel and cut parsnips into slices about ¾ inch (2 cm) thick. Place in 1½ cups (375 ml) of boiling water; simmer for 10 to 15 minutes or until parsnips are tender. Remove from heat and cool slightly.
2. Place 1 cup (250 g) of the cooked parsnips and ½ cup (125 ml) of the cooking water into the blender. Puree. Repeat with the remaining vegetable. Pour into ice-cube trays and freeze.

Yield
2 ice-cube trays

Storage Life
6 months

Parsnips are a good source of vitamin A.

Puree of Beetroot

1 lb. (500 g) beetroot
(approximately 6 small beetroot)
Water
Preparation
1. Wash beetroot, cut stalks off 2 inches (5 cm) from the top of the vegetable; do not peel beetroot.
2. Place unpeeled beetroot into 1 cup (250 ml) of boiling water. Simmer for 30 to 60 minutes or until beetroots are tender (age and size of beetroot affect cooking time). Remove from heat and cool slightly.
3. Peel and slice cooked beetroot. Place into the blender. Add ¼ to ⅓ cup (60 to 85 ml) of fresh water, not the cooking water. Puree. Pour into ice-cube trays and freeze.

Yield
1 ice-cube tray
Storage Life
6 months
Comments
Whole beetroot can also be cooked in the pressure cooker or steamed before they are pureed; well-drained canned beetroot may also be used. When beetroot is served, a bib for both mother and baby is a good idea. Serve this vegetable after six months of age and only occasionally.

Mixed Vegetable Puree

Ingredients
1 lb (500 g) mixed vegetables (4 carrots, 4 parsnips, sliced)
1 lb (500 g) peeled and sliced potatoes (2 average potatoes)
Water
Preparation
1. Peel and cut the vegetables into pieces; place all vegetables, except the potatoes, into 1 cup (250 ml) of boiling water. Simmer for 10 minutes. Add the potatoes and simmer until all vegetables are tender (about 20 minutes). Remove from heat and cool slightly.

2. Place into the blender ½ lb (250 g) of the cooked vegetables and about ⅓ cup (85 ml) of the cooking water. Puree. Repeat with the remaining vegetables. Pour into ice-cube trays and freeze.

Yield

2 ice-cube trays

Storage Life

6 months

Comments

Carrots and parsnips can be replaced by turnip, swede or another root vegetable.

NOTE: This puree should be served only after each individual vegetable has been introduced to the baby first.

Puree of Marrow

Ingredients

1 marrow

Water

Preparation

1. Bake the whole marrow in a 350°F (180°C) oven for about 1½ hours. Once cooked, cut in half and remove seeds and skin.
2. Place the fleshy part of the marrow and a small amount of water (60 ml or more) into the blender. Puree. Pour into ice-cube trays and freeze.

Yield

1 ice-cube tray or more depending on the size of the marrow.

Storage Life

6 months

Comments

Frozen marrow can be used in this recipe. The whole marrow family supplies good quantities of vitamin A.

Marrow and Apple Puree

Ingredients

¾ lb (375 g) fresh marrow cut into pieces

3 to 4 apples, peeled and sliced

Water

Preparation
1. Place apples and pieces of marrow into 1 cup (250 ml) of boiling water. Simmer for 25 to 30 minutes or until tender. Remove from heat and cool slightly.
2. Place half of the apple-marrow mixture into the blender along with ⅓ cup (85 ml) of the cooking water. Puree. Repeat with the remaining ingredients. Pour into ice-cube trays and freeze.

Yield
2 ice-cube trays
Storage Life
6 months
Comments
A pleasant way to eat marrow, a vegetable which provides an excellent source of vitamin A.

Puree of Courgettes

Ingredients
1½ lb. (700 g) young courgettes
(7 to 8 small ones)
Water
Preparation
1. Peel and slice courgettes. Place into 1 cup of boiling water or into a steamer. Simmer gently for about 15 minutes. Remove from heat, drain well, and cool slightly.
2. Place into the blender without any water. Puree. Repeat with the remaining cooked courgettes.
3. Pour into ice-cube trays and freeze.

Yield
2 ice-cube trays
Storage Life
6 months
Comments
Courgettes are sweet and pleasant tasting. The puree appears as a pretty spring green.

Puree of Celery

Ingredients
1 lb. (500 g) tender and young celery (in season)

Water

1 tablespoon of unsalted butter or margarine

Preparation

1. Wash and cut celery into 2 inch (5 cm) pieces. Place into about ½ cup (125 ml) of boiling water. Simmer for 10 to 15 minutes or until the celery is tender. Remove from heat and cool slightly.
2. Place into the blender half of the celery and a small amount of cooking water. Puree. Repeat with the remaining celery. Add butter or margarine to the puree. Pour into ice-cube trays and freeze.

Yield

1 ice-cube tray

Storage Life

6 months

Puree of Cauliflower

Ingredients

1 small head of cauliflower

Water

½ cup (125 ml) of whole milk*

Preparation

1. Section the cauliflower into small florets. Place into 1 cup (250 ml) of boiling water. Simmer for 10 to 15 minutes or until the cauliflower is tender. Remove from heat and cool slightly.
2. Place into the blender with 1½ cups (375 ml) of the cooking water and half the milk. Puree. Repeat with the remaining ingredients. Pour into ice-cube trays and freeze.

Yield

2 ice-cube trays, depending on the size of the cauliflower

Storage Life

4 to 6 weeks

Comments

Cauliflower absorbs a lot of liquid while cooking; this is the reason for adding milk when making the puree.

As with all members of the cabbage family, cauliflower is rich in vitamin C.

*Do not give semi-skimmed or skimmed milk to a baby under one year of age.

Puree of Broccoli

Ingredients
1 bunch of fresh (green) broccoli (5 to 6 stalks)
Water
Preparation
1. Cut the stalks and retain only the flower part of the broccoli for baby purees (the stalks may be cooked and served along with another vegetable to the rest of the family).
2. Place the pieces of broccoli into 1 cup (250 ml) of boiling water. Simmer for 10 minutes or until the broccoli is tender but still very green. Remove from heat and cool slightly.
3. Place half of the broccoli along with (60 ml) of the cooking water into the blender. Puree. Repeat with the remaining broccoli. Pour into ice-cube trays and freeze.

Yield
1 ice-cube tray
Storage Life
6 months
Comments
Fresh and bright green broccoli has a sweet and pleasant flavour. It is rich in vitamins A and C. It also contains iron and calcium.

Apple Sauce

Ingredients
8 to 10 medium apples
Water
Cinnamon (optional)
Preparation
1. Wash apples well. Remove cores, cut into quarters, and slice. Place apples in a saucepan with ½ cup (125 ml) of water. Bring to the boil, reduce heat and simmer for about 15 minutes or until apples are tender.
2. Remove from heat and cool slightly.
3. Place 2 cups (500 ml) of the cooked apples into the blender and puree until the peel has completely disappeared. (If the blender is not powerful enough to pulverize the peel entirely, pass the puree through a sieve or peel apples before cooking.)
4. Repeat with the remaining apples.
5. If desired, a pinch of cinnamon may be added to the puree.

6. Pour into ice-cube trays and freeze.
Yield
2 ice-cube trays
Storage Life
6 to 8 months
Comments
Cooking time may vary according to the type of apple used.

Puree of Pear

Ingredients
9 to 11 medium pears (fresh)
½ cup (125 ml) water or apple juice
Preparation
1. Peel pears, quarter and core.
2. Place into a saucepan with ½ cup (125 ml) of water or apple juice. Simmer for 15 to 20 minutes or until pears are tender. Remove from heat and cool slightly.
3. Place half of the cooked pears into the blender with ⅛ cup (20 ml) of the cooking liquid. Puree. Repeat with the remaining pears.
4. Pour puree into ice-cube trays and freeze.
Yield
2 ice-cube trays
Storage Life
6 to 8 months
Comments
If canned pears are used, they should be carefully rinsed to eliminate as much sugar as possible; they should not be cooked. However, unsweetened pears canned in their natural juice are now available; this juice may be used as the liquid in the making of the puree.

Puree of Pear and Apple

Ingredients
5 apples and 5 pears
½ cup (125 ml) water or apple juice
Preparation
1. Peel apples and pears; quarter and core them.

126

2. Place into a saucepan with the water or the apple juice and simmer for 15 to 20 minutes or until the apples and pears are tender.
3. Remove from heat and cool slightly.
4. Place half the fruit into the blender with about ¼ cup (60 ml) of the cooking liquid. Puree. Repeat with the remaining fruit.
5. Pour into ice-cube trays.

Yield
2 ice-cube trays

Storage Life
6 to 8 months

Comments
The amounts of liquid may vary depending on the type of apples and pears used.
    A fruit puree can be made by mashing cooked fruit with a fork.

Puree of Peach

Ingredients
2 lbs (1 kilo) fresh peaches, peeled, pitted, and sliced
⅓ to ½ cup (85 to 125 ml) water

Preparation
1. Put peaches and water into a saucepan. Bring to the boil, reduce heat and simmer gently for about 15 to 20 minutes or until peaches are tender.
2. Remove from heat and cool slightly.
3. Place 2 cups (500 ml) of cooked peaches into the blender together with a very small amount of the cooking water. Puree.
4. Repeat with the remaining peaches.
5. Pour into ice-cube trays and freeze.

Yield
2 ice-cube trays

Storage Life
6 to 8 months

Comments
Avoid adding too much water when blending. The amount required will depend on the type of peaches used. If canned peaches are used, they must be rinsed well in order to eliminate as much of the sugar as possible. They do not have to be cooked before blending. Peaches canned in grape or unsweetened fruit

juice are also available on the market. This liquid may be used to
replace the cooking water when making the puree.

Puree of Apricot

Ingredients
2 lbs (1 kilo) unpeeled fresh apricots, pitted and sliced
½ cup (125 ml) water
Preparation
1. Place apricots and water into a saucepan. Bring to the boil,
   reduce heat. Simmer for about 15 mintutes or until fruit is
   tender.
2. Remove from heat and cool slightly.
3. Place half of the apricots into the blender with about ¼ cup
   (60 ml) of the cooking water. Puree. Repeat with the remaining
   apricots.
4. Pour into ice-cube trays and freeze.
Yield
2 ice-cube trays
Storage Life
6 to 8 months
Comments
As with peaches, do not add too much water when blending.
One part of the apricots may be replaced with either apples or
pears – 1 lb (500 g) pears, (1 lb 500 g) apricots. Again, canned
apricots which have been carefully rinsed may be used but do not
cook. Apricots are a good source of vitamin A.

Puree of Prune and Apple

Ingredients
¾ lb (350 g) pitted prunes
2 cups (500 ml) hot water
1 lb (500 g) peeled, sliced, cored apples
1½ cups (375 ml) cold water
Preparation
1. Soak prunes in hot water for 5 to 15 minutes; drain.
2. Place prunes, apples, and cold water into a saucepan; bring to
   the boil; reduce heat and simmer for about 20 minutes.

3. Remove from heat and cool slightly.
4. Place half of the prunes and apples and about $\frac{1}{2}$ cup (125 ml) of the cooking water into the blender. Puree. Repeat with the remaining fruit.
5. Pour into ice-cube trays.

Yield
2 ice-cube trays

Storage Life
6 months

Comments
This puree could be the solution in the case of an infant who is constipated and does not eliminate regularly.

If the prunes when purchased are not pitted, the pits are easily removed after the 15-minute soak. When mashed with a fork, the fruit resembles a puree.

Puree of Lamb

Ingredients
1 lb. (500 g) boneless lean lamb, cut in $1\frac{1}{2}$ inch (4 cm) cubes
3 carrots, peeled and cut into pieces
2 potatoes, peeled and quartered
1 tablespoon (15 g) minced onion
1 stalk of celery, cut into pieces
Water

Preparation
1. Place all ingredients into a saucepan with 2 cups (500 ml) of water. Bring to the boil; reduce heat. Simmer for approximately 45 minutes, or until lamb and vegetables are tender. Remove from heat and cool slightly.
2. Separate the cooked lamb from the vegetables. Place half the meat and $\frac{1}{2}$ cup (125 ml) of the stock into the blender. Puree. Repeat with remaining lamb.
3. Pour into ice-cube trays and freeze.

Yield
12 small cubes

Storage Life
10 to 12 weeks

Comments
The vegetables may also be pureed with a small amount of lamb to produce a vegetable and lamb dinner.

Puree of Beef

Ingredients
1 lb. (500 g) lean, tender beef (top or sirloin) cut into 1 inch
(2.5 cm) cubes
1 stalk of celery cut into pieces
3 carrots, peeled and cut into pieces
2 medium potatoes, peeled and quartered
1 tablespoon (15 g) minced onion
Water
Preparation
1. Place beef and 2¼ cups (560 ml) of water into a saucepan;
   simmer for about 45 minutes.
2. Add celery, carrots and potatoes and cook for an additional 35
   to 40 minutes, or until all ingredients are tender. Remove from
   heat and cool slightly.
3. Separate the beef from the vegetables and place 180 g of the
   meat into the blender with ⅓ cup (85 ml) of the stock. Puree.
   Repeat with remaining beef. Pour into ice-cube trays and
   freeze.
Yield
12 small cubes
Storage Life
10 to 12 weeks
Comments
The vegetables may be pureed with a small amount of beef to
make a 'vegetable and beef' dinner.

Puree of Chicken Livers

Ingredients
5 to 6 chicken livers
Unsalted chicken stock (homemade)
Preparation
1. Prepare livers for cooking by cutting and removing the white
   membrane; cut livers in half. Place into a saucepan with 1 cup
   (250 ml) of unsalted chicken stock. Bring to the boil; reduce
   heat immediately. Simmer 5 to 10 minutes, or until chicken
   livers are cooked (grey-brown inside). Remove from heat and
   cool slightly.
2. Place a few chicken livers into the blender with a small amount

of cooking liquid. Puree. Repeat with remaining liver.

3. Pour into ice-cube trays and freeze.

Yield
6 cubes

Storage Life
10 to 12 weeks

Comments
Liver is an excellent source of iron and protein. Chicken livers have a milder flavour than other types of liver. With a small amount of carrot or another favourite vegetable, it's a guaranteed success.

Puree of Chicken

Ingredients
1 chicken, 2 to 3 lb. (1 to 1.3 kg) cut into 4 to 8 pieces
1 stalk of celery cut into pieces
1 tablespoon (15 g) minced onion
1 sprig of parsley
3 carrots, peeled and cut into pieces
1 medium potato, peeled and quartered

Preparation
1. Place chicken, celery, onion and parsley into a saucepan. Add 3 cups (750 ml) of water. Simmer for 40 to 50 minutes.
2. Add the vegetables (carrots and potato). Simmer for an additional 40 to 45 minutes or until the chicken is cooked and the meat separates easily from the bones.
3. Remove from heat and cool slightly.
4. Remove the meat from the bones and cut into small pieces. Place 125 g of chicken and ⅓ cup (85 ml) of the stock into the blender. Puree. Repeat with remaining chicken.
5. Pour puree into ice-cube trays and freeze.

Yield
One tray of cubes or more, depending on the size of the chicken.

Storage Life
10 to 12 weeks

Comments
Turkey can easily replace chicken in the recipe; frozen turkey halves or quarters can be purchased and cooked in the same manner as the chicken.

NOTE: The vegetables may be pureed with a small amount of chicken to make a vegetable and chicken dinner.

Puree of Fish

Ingredients
2 white fish fillets (sole, cod, plaice, haddock) 8 oz. (200 g) approximately
1 to 2 tablespoons (15 to 30 g) finely minced onion
½ cup (125 ml) whole milk *

Preparation
1. Pour ¼ cup (60 ml) of milk into a frying pan and heat gently. Add the onion; cook for a few minutes.
2. Add the fish fillets. Cover with a lid or aluminium foil. Cook over slow heat for 5 to 10 minutes or until the fish is very white and flakes easily with a fork. Remove from heat and cool slightly.
3. Place half of the fish and the milk used in cooking into the blender. Blend until smooth; add more milk if necessary. Repeat with the remaining fish. Pour into ice-cube trays and freeze.

Yield
8 cubes

Storage Life
4 to 6 weeks

Comments
White fish is an excellent source of protein. It contains less fat than meat and its preparation is faster. It has a mild and pleasant flavour.

*Do not give skimmed or semi-skimmed milk to a baby under one year of age.

132

CHAPTER ELEVEN

Some Very Special Flowers
Talk About Nutrition

TRANSLATING VITAMINS and minerals into daily nutritional needs is not that complicated. In order to ease the process and to better understand the different nutritional needs of the young child, this chapter presents a summary of fourteen essential nutrients.

Each flower represents a specific nutrient and the parts of each flower reveal pertinent nutritional information. The heart of the flower represents its role, while the petals indicate the major food sources of the nutrient. The leaves represent the child's daily needs both in technical terms and in terms of actual food portions. How cooking affects the nutrient completes the information.

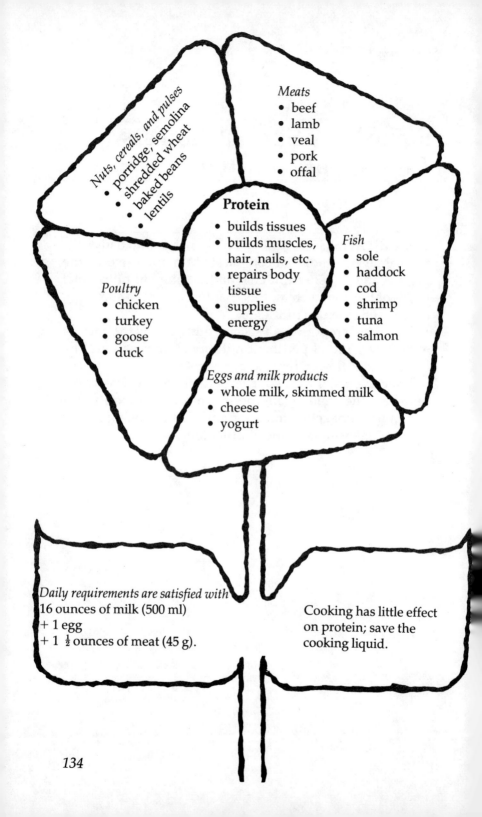

Nuts, cereals, and pulses
- porridge, semolina
- shredded wheat
- baked beans
- lentils

Meats
- beef
- lamb
- veal
- pork
- offal

Protein
- builds tissues
- builds muscles, hair, nails, etc.
- repairs body tissue
- supplies energy

Fish
- sole
- haddock
- cod
- shrimp
- tuna
- salmon

Poultry
- chicken
- turkey
- goose
- duck

Eggs and milk products
- whole milk, skimmed milk
- cheese
- yogurt

Daily requirements are satisfied with
16 ounces of milk (500 ml)
+ 1 egg
+ 1 ½ ounces of meat (45 g).

Cooking has little effect on protein; save the cooking liquid.

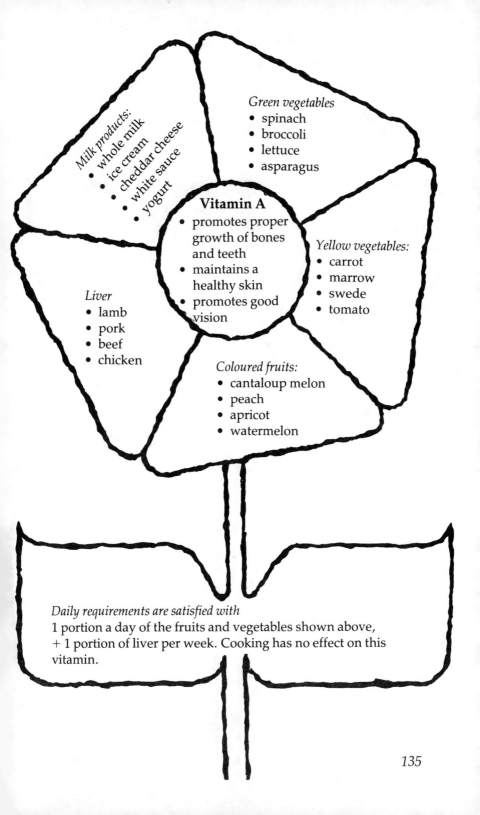

Vitamin A
- promotes proper growth of bones and teeth
- maintains a healthy skin
- promotes good vision

Milk products:
- whole milk
- ice cream
- cheddar cheese
- white sauce
- yogurt

Green vegetables
- spinach
- broccoli
- lettuce
- asparagus

Yellow vegetables:
- carrot
- marrow
- swede
- tomato

Liver
- lamb
- pork
- beef
- chicken

Coloured fruits:
- cantaloup melon
- peach
- apricot
- watermelon

Daily requirements are satisfied with
1 portion a day of the fruits and vegetables shown above,
+ 1 portion of liver per week. Cooking has no effect on this vitamin.

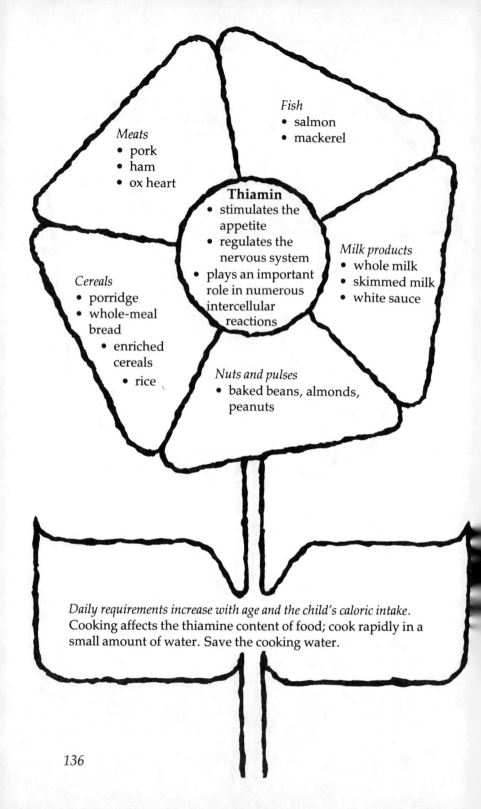

Meats
• pork
• ham
• ox heart

Fish
• salmon
• mackerel

Thiamin
• stimulates the appetite
• regulates the nervous system
• plays an important role in numerous intercellular reactions

Milk products
• whole milk
• skimmed milk
• white sauce

Cereals
• porridge
• whole-meal bread
• enriched cereals
• rice

Nuts and pulses
• baked beans, almonds, peanuts

Daily requirements increase with age and the child's caloric intake. Cooking affects the thiamine content of food; cook rapidly in a small amount of water. Save the cooking water.

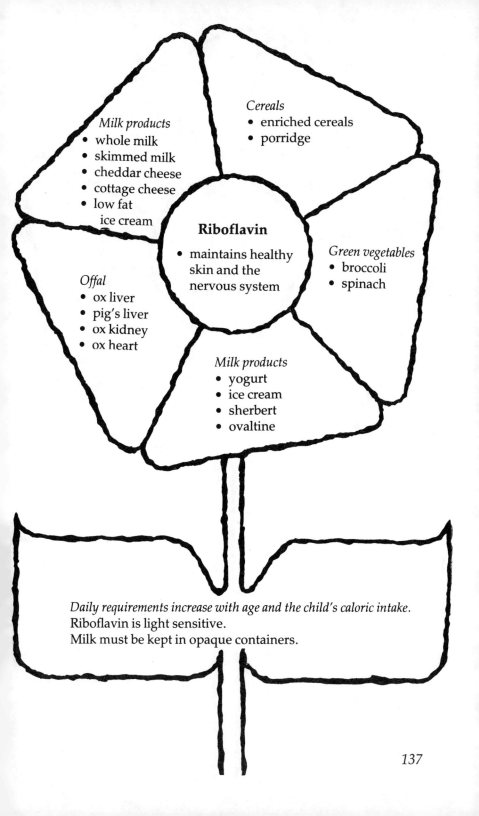

Milk products
- whole milk
- skimmed milk
- cheddar cheese
- cottage cheese
- low fat
  ice cream

Cereals
- enriched cereals
- porridge

Riboflavin
- maintains healthy skin and the nervous system

Green vegetables
- broccoli
- spinach

Offal
- ox liver
- pig's liver
- ox kidney
- ox heart

Milk products
- yogurt
- ice cream
- sherbert
- ovaltine

Daily requirements increase with age and the child's caloric intake.
Riboflavin is light sensitive.
Milk must be kept in opaque containers.

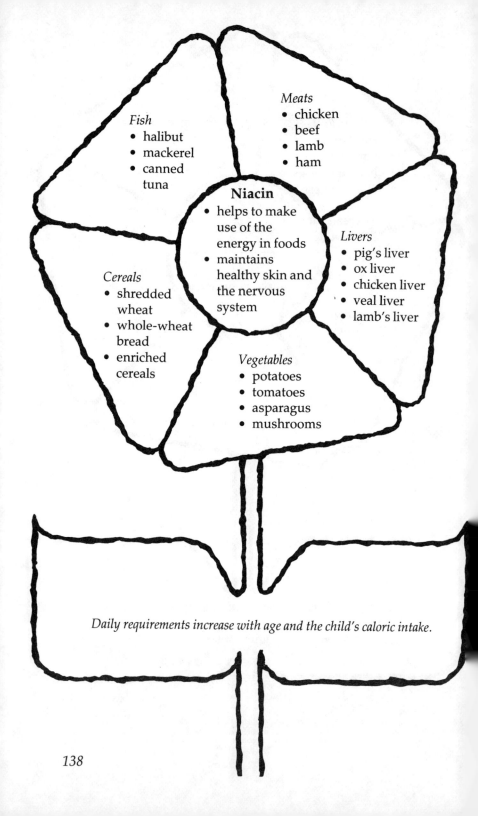

Fish
- halibut
- mackerel
- canned tuna

Meats
- chicken
- beef
- lamb
- ham

Niacin
- helps to make use of the energy in foods
- maintains healthy skin and the nervous system

Livers
- pig's liver
- ox liver
- chicken liver
- veal liver
- lamb's liver

Cereals
- shredded wheat
- whole-wheat bread
- enriched cereals

Vegetables
- potatoes
- tomatoes
- asparagus
- mushrooms

Daily requirements increase with age and the child's caloric intake.

Meats
- roast beef
- veal
- lamb

Offal
- ox liver
- ox heart
- chicken liver
- kidneys
- pig's liver

Vitamin B ^{12}
- plays a role in numerous inter-cellular reactions
- participates in the development of red blood cells and nerve tissue

Fish
- canned salmon
- mackerel

Eggs and milk products
- whole or skimmed milk
- cottage cheese
- fine cheese
- eggs

Daily requirements are satisfied with
1 portion of meat/day or 2 cups of milk/day (500 ml).
Vitamin B ^{12} is not affected by normal cooking procedures.

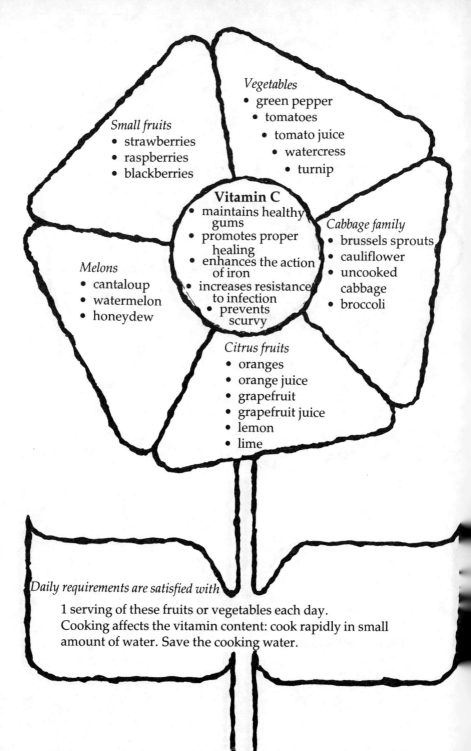

Vegetables
- green pepper
- tomatoes
- tomato juice
- watercress
- turnip

Small fruits
- strawberries
- raspberries
- blackberries

Vitamin C
- maintains healthy gums
- promotes proper healing
- enhances the action of iron
- increases resistance to infection
- prevents scurvy

Cabbage family
- brussels sprouts
- cauliflower
- uncooked cabbage
- broccoli

Melons
- cantaloup
- watermelon
- honeydew

Citrus fruits
- oranges
- orange juice
- grapefruit
- grapefruit juice
- lemon
- lime

Daily requirements are satisfied with

1 serving of these fruits or vegetables each day.
Cooking affects the vitamin content: cook rapidly in small amount of water. Save the cooking water.

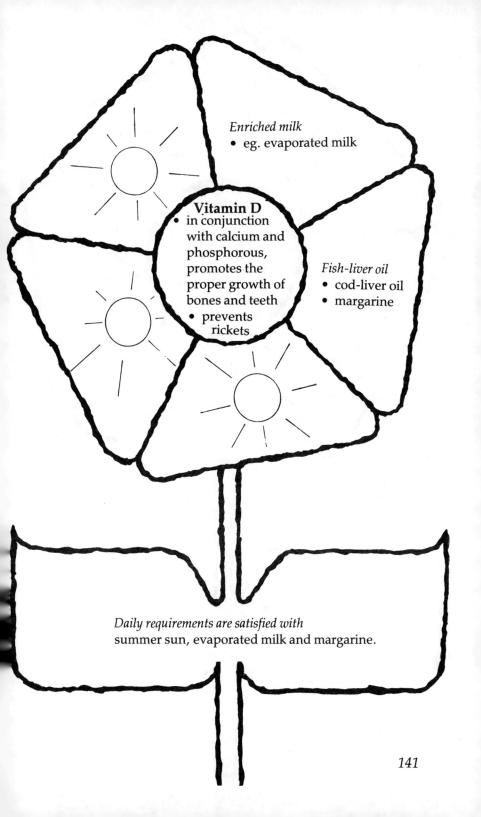

Vitamin D
- in conjunction with calcium and phosphorous, promotes the proper growth of bones and teeth
- prevents rickets

Enriched milk
- eg. evaporated milk

Fish-liver oil
- cod-liver oil
- margarine

Daily requirements are satisfied with summer sun, evaporated milk and margarine.

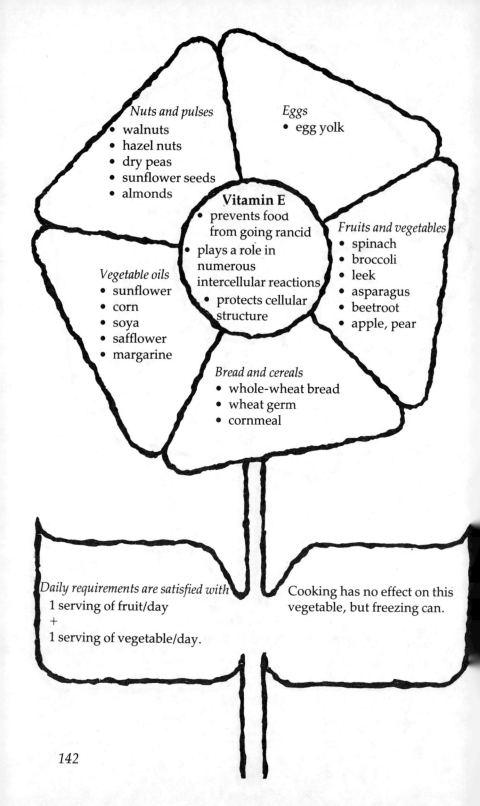

Nuts and pulses
- walnuts
- hazel nuts
- dry peas
- sunflower seeds
- almonds

Eggs
- egg yolk

Vitamin E
- prevents food from going rancid
- plays a role in numerous intercellular reactions
- protects cellular structure

Fruits and vegetables
- spinach
- broccoli
- leek
- asparagus
- beetroot
- apple, pear

Vegetable oils
- sunflower
- corn
- soya
- safflower
- margarine

Bread and cereals
- whole-wheat bread
- wheat germ
- cornmeal

Daily requirements are satisfied with
1 serving of fruit/day
+
1 serving of vegetable/day.

Cooking has no effect on this vegetable, but freezing can.

142

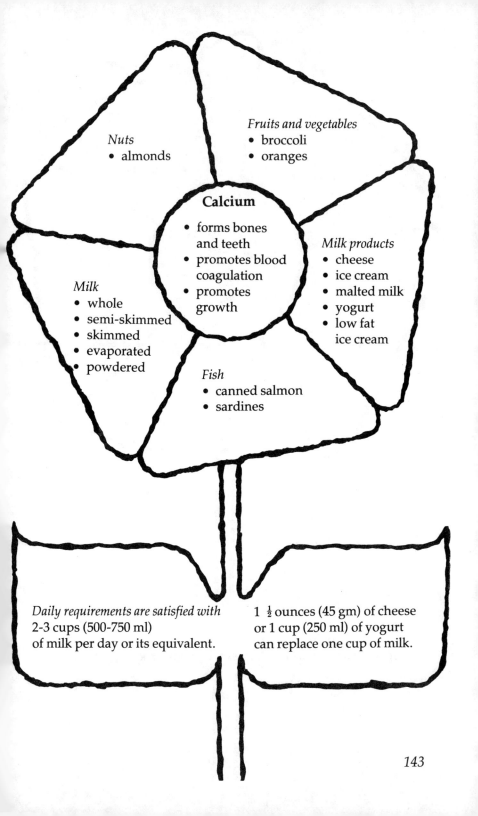

Nuts
- almonds

Fruits and vegetables
- broccoli
- oranges

Calcium
- forms bones and teeth
- promotes blood coagulation
- promotes growth

Milk products
- cheese
- ice cream
- malted milk
- yogurt
- low fat ice cream

Milk
- whole
- semi-skimmed
- skimmed
- evaporated
- powdered

Fish
- canned salmon
- sardines

Daily requirements are satisfied with 2-3 cups (500-750 ml) of milk per day or its equivalent.

1 ½ ounces (45 gm) of cheese or 1 cup (250 ml) of yogurt can replace one cup of milk.

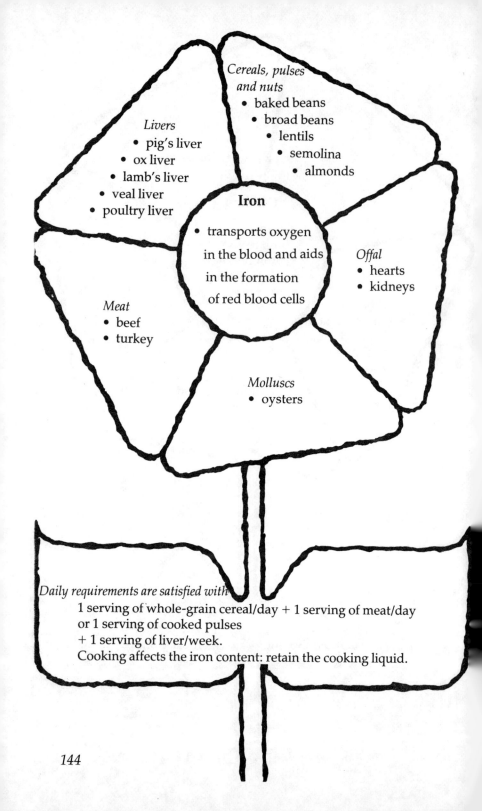

Cereals, pulses
and nuts
- baked beans
- broad beans
- lentils
- semolina
- almonds

Livers
- pig's liver
- ox liver
- lamb's liver
- veal liver
- poultry liver

Iron
- transports oxygen
in the blood and aids
in the formation
of red blood cells

Offal
- hearts
- kidneys

Meat
- beef
- turkey

Molluscs
- oysters

Daily requirements are satisfied with
1 serving of whole-grain cereal/day + 1 serving of meat/day
or 1 serving of cooked pulses
+ 1 serving of liver/week.
Cooking affects the iron content: retain the cooking liquid.

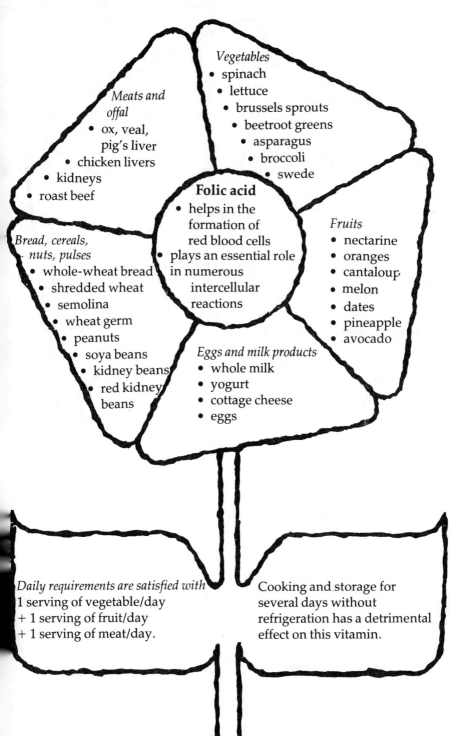

Vegetables
- spinach
- lettuce
- brussels sprouts
- beetroot greens
- asparagus
- broccoli
- swede

Meats and offal
- ox, veal, pig's liver
- chicken livers
- kidneys
- roast beef

Folic acid
- helps in the formation of red blood cells
- plays an essential role in numerous intercellular reactions

Fruits
- nectarine
- oranges
- cantaloup
- melon
- dates
- pineapple
- avocado

Bread, cereals, nuts, pulses
- whole-wheat bread
- shredded wheat
- semolina
- wheat germ
- peanuts
- soya beans
- kidney beans
- red kidney beans

Eggs and milk products
- whole milk
- yogurt
- cottage cheese
- eggs

Daily requirements are satisfied with 1 serving of vegetable/day + 1 serving of fruit/day + 1 serving of meat/day.

Cooking and storage for several days without refrigeration has a detrimental effect on this vitamin.

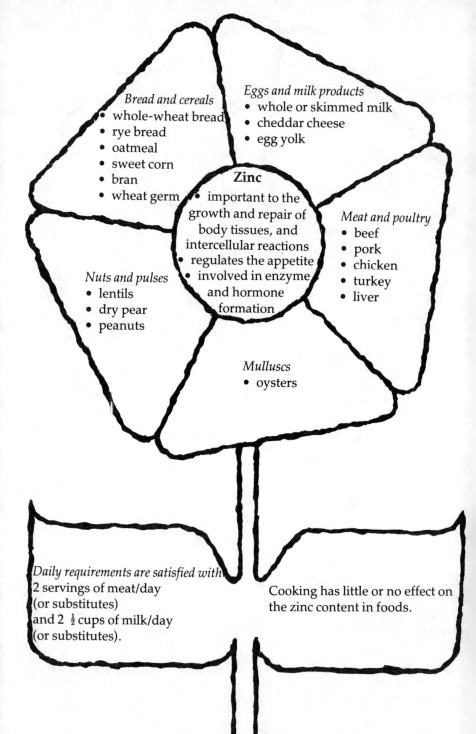

Bread and cereals
- whole-wheat bread
- rye bread
- oatmeal
- sweet corn
- bran
- wheat germ

Eggs and milk products
- whole or skimmed milk
- cheddar cheese
- egg yolk

Zinc
- important to the growth and repair of body tissues, and intercellular reactions
- regulates the appetite
- involved in enzyme and hormone formation

Meat and poultry
- beef
- pork
- chicken
- turkey
- liver

Nuts and pulses
- lentils
- dry pear
- peanuts

Mulluscs
- oysters

Daily requirements are satisfied with 2 servings of meat/day (or substitutes) and 2 ½ cups of milk/day (or substitutes).

Cooking has little or no effect on the zinc content in foods.

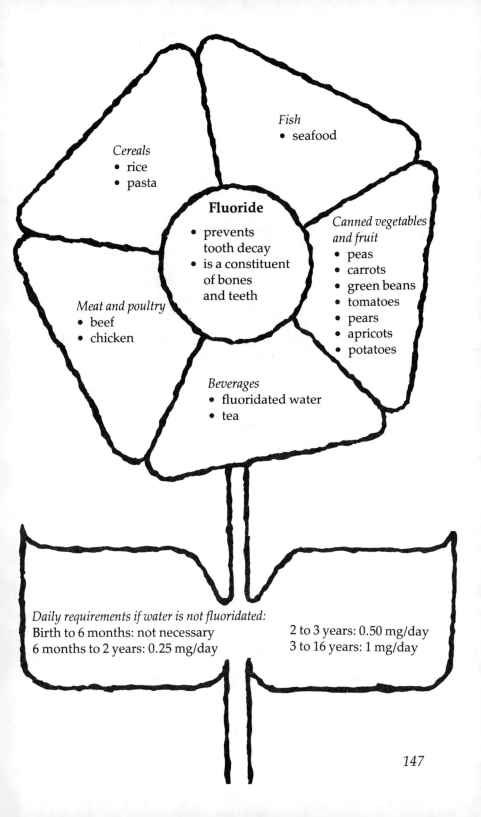

Fish
- seafood

Cereals
- rice
- pasta

Fluoride
- prevents tooth decay
- is a constituent of bones and teeth

Canned vegetables and fruit
- peas
- carrots
- green beans
- tomatoes
- pears
- apricots
- potatoes

Meat and poultry
- beef
- chicken

Beverages
- fluoridated water
- tea

Daily requirements if water is not fluoridated:
Birth to 6 months: not necessary
6 months to 2 years: 0.25 mg/day

2 to 3 years: 0.50 mg/day
3 to 16 years: 1 mg/day

CHAPTER TWELVE

A Child's Diet After Nine Months of Age

FEEDING A CHILD between nine months and six years of age never ceases to interest, if not torment, many parents. Poor parents! We have the uncanny knack of making mountains out of molehills. Unintentionally, we jeopardize the harmonious development of our child's healthy eating habits by misinterpreting his unpredictable behaviour:

- 'At six months, our child ate so well. Now at twenty months, he refuses to eat practically everything.'
- 'Mealtime is the most difficult time of my entire day.'
- 'My two-and-a-half-year-old daughter eats only peanut butter sandwiches day in and day out.'
- 'My three-and-a-half-year-old son would rather play with his food than eat it.'
- 'Mine refuses to eat vegetables. Any vegetables.'

Surprising Fact — A child who eats too little arouses five times as much attention as one who eats too much.

Alarming Fact — Parents attach an importance to food which goes far beyond its true value; food is often used as a vehicle for reward and punishment, or as a means of bargaining.

- 'If you don't finish your meat, you can't have any ice cream.'
- 'No dessert for you. You hit your sister.'
- 'Eat your green beans and you can have some dessert.'

The 'reward' foods are nearly always desserts, cakes, or sweets. The foods withheld as punishment are also desserts, cakes, and sweets.

This sugar-pleasure-reward association, reinforced by

the child's environmental experiences, are bound to remain with him for a long time.

Important Fact — Healthy food attitudes are acquired around the table. Eating habits of parents have a tremendous influence on the child's own eating behaviour.

A father who consistently refuses to eat broccoli, liver and fish will have a hard time convincing his child to eat these foods. Can a mother who skips breakfast reprimand her children for wanting to do the same?

The pleasure a family experiences in eating a wide variety of foods is contagious and easily transmitted to a child. Inversely, new food experiences are rarely sought by a child brought up in an environment where food is perceived as a necessity and served in a routine and monotonous manner.

Without denying the preschool child's fluctuations in appetite, patience and understanding can help circumvent the problem. The acceptance of a few food whims is much better in the long run than daily confrontation around problem foods.

Respect for a child's appetite and the development of good eating habits begun in the early months of life must continue in spite of the odd problem encountered during the formative years. A better understanding of the total development of a child (physical growth, motor and social skills) will aid in the acceptance of appetite fluctuations.

Revealing Fact — The younger the child, the more willing he will be to try new foods. Seventy-seven percent of children between one and two years of age will try new foods. This percentage drops to 10% in children between two and four years of age, and to 7% in children four years of age and older.

A child who is taught to eat a variety of foods at a very young age will continue to derive much pleasure in diversifying his diet for the rest of his life.

It should be remembered that the preschool child's eating habits, his appetite fluctuations and his whims, indicate on the one hand a slowing of his growth, and on the other hand an assertion of his personality and independence.

The Child's Point of View

A child wants to eat when he is hungry. Food brings him comfort and both physical and emotional satisfaction.

A child does not come into the world with eating habits already established. As we have seen previously, these habits are formed slowly but surely during the first years of life.

Along with the food he eats, a child receives messages which enable him to shape his attitudes and feelings about the whole process of eating. A child who has been fed with love will love to eat, but a child who has been fed with impatience and indifference will not have such a positive attitude towards his food. It is partly through his meals that a child makes contact with the outside world as it begins to play an ever-increasing part in his life. Towards the age of one he begins to express his preferences clearly and reacts to the texture, temperature, taste and colour of his food, to the size of the helping he is given, and to the general atmosphere of the meal. If he refuses a dish, it is because one or more of these aspects displeases him.

His Tastes

Although no two children react in exactly the same way, common factors are nonetheless discernible in the pre-school child.

Texture

He likes his food to be soft in consistency and not dry and hard. He really enjoys puddings which are runnier than usual, and cooked cereals which are less stodgy; he prefers mashed potatoes to a baked potato, minced meat to steaks, and fresh bread to dry bread. These food preferences are due in part to the fact that at this age the child has little saliva, which would normally act as a lubricant.

Temperature

He likes to be served food which is lukewarm, soup which has cooled off, ice cream which has softened, milk at room temperature, etc.

Flavour

He prefers mild flavours and he reacts to the slightest flavour changes – milk which is almost sour, and slightly over-cooked vegetables. Spicy and seasoned foods are unpopular, unless his cultural background encourages this type of dish. An Italian child will appreciate the flavour of garlic and onions more than his Northern European counterpart.

Colour

He likes colours and colour contrasts. A bright dish (chicken, carrots, and broccoli) produces a positive reaction, while a dull dish (fish, mashed potatoes and butter beans) will not stimulate his appetite; on the contrary it might well deaden it. A child eats first with his eyes, more so than an adult. Colours fascinate him, whether they are on the plate or on the table: red place mats, striped napkins, a garnish of parsley on the potato, a green pepper ring on the tomatoes, a fruit salad of cantaloup melon and green grapes – there are so many ways of adding colour to the table and pleasing the eyes of little ones.

Portion Size

Plates containing miniature portions get a better response from the child; one filled to the brim discourages him before he even starts. It is wiser to give him the pleasure of coming back for seconds than to force him to leave a half-filled plate. Food prepared in bite-size pieces is more appealing and easier to handle. A child must be given the chance to master the situation.

Mealtime Atmosphere

A calm and relaxed atmosphere helps the child to eat well. Loud background noise should be turned off at mealtime: the washer, the dryer, the fan, a blaring radio, the television set, etc. A child's attention cannot be split the same way as an adult's; he can only do one thing at a time. When noises or lively conversations are present at mealtime, he forgets to eat. A favourable atmosphere, on the other hand, encourages the acceptance of a new food.

Furthermore, the child likes to see what he is eating; he inspects his food. He will often pull a sandwich apart or break up a casserole simply to find out what foods are in it. He doesn't like mixtures. This is the simple food stage when food is easy to see, to handle and to eat.

His Aptitudes

Knowing a preschool child's pattern of chronological motor, physical, and social development, enables us to understand better his eating behaviour.

XII-1: *The Preschool Child's Motor and Social Aptitudes*

Age	Manual Abilities	Physical and Social Behaviour
6 to 12 months	• uses hands	• displays interest in texture and consistency • discovery through smell, handling

15 months	• grasps spoon, places it on the plate, but fills it improperly • holds spoon upside-down close to mouth • often drops cup and spoon	• slight decrease in appetite • everything goes into the mouth
18 months	• drinks well from the cup but has difficulty putting it down • turns the spoon in his mouth	• growth rate slows • appetite decreases considerably • loves rituals
2 years	• drinks from a small glass held in one hand • puts spoon in mouth without turning it	• pulls objects apart and asks for help • learns to say 'no' • begins to show whims and specific and monotonous preferences
3 years	• can pour liquids from a small container • rarely asks for help • uses a fork • makes little mess	• whims less apparent • more accommodating in his attitude
4 years	• uses a fork and a knife	• displays whims and goes on 'hunger strikes' • able to set the table

| 5 years | • still prefers simple foods | • accepts new situation more readily |
| | | • is influenced by others |

His 'Arrhythmical' Growth

During the first year of life, a child grows approximately 10 inches (25 cm), and triples his birth weight. It's a once-in-a-lifetime accomplishment. Throughout the preschool years, the child continues to grow but he adds only 16 to 17 inches (40 cm) to his height, and 23 pounds (10 kg) to his weight in the entire five years. After the first year, the yearly growth rate is about three to four inches (8 cm), and around four pounds (1.7 kg). The growth rate is slowing down.

XII-2: *A Child's Growth Rate*

	Birth	One Year	Six Years
BOYS			
height	20 in.	30 in.	46 in.
	(50 cm)	(75 cm)	(115 cm)
weight	7.5 lb.	23 lb.	45 lb.
	(3.3 kg)	(10 kg)	(19.8 kg)
GIRLS			
height	19 in.	29 in.	46 in.
	(48.5 cm)	(73.5 cm)	(115 cm)
weight	7.3 lb.	22 lb.	46 lb.
	(3.2 kg)	(10 kg)	(20 kg)

This obvious slowdown in growth is the reason for the preschool child's decrease in appetite. The eight-month-old baby who happily gobbles up everything in sight is growing at an almost visible rate, while the whimsical two-and-a-half-year-old hardly grows at all.

On the other hand, unexpected and unpredictable growth spurts account for the fluctuation in appetite during these early years. Suddenly the child grows in height, stops, puts on weight, then stops again. These intermittent growth spurts are accompanied by a temporary increase in appetite. Between these two growth spurts the appetite decreases. There is no need whatever to worry about this.

Despite these variations in his growth and appetite, the young child has special nutritional needs that must be met if the specific demands of his body are to be satisfied. The formation of his muscles, bones and blood calls for an adequate consumption of foods rich in protein, calcium, phosphorous, vitamin D and iron. Resistance to infections and the overall healthy functioning of the body necessitates adequate intake of foods rich in vitamins A, B, and C.

A varied, well-balanced diet is one of the keys to a child's health.

Food Choices at Different Ages

The preschool child adapts gradually to a varied diet and discovers new foods month after month. His diet is made up of basic foods which are prepared in various ways according to his capabilities. The evolution of the diet parallels the child's development, both physiologically and physically.

The following pages suggest a choice of foods adapted to various age groups and indicate the quantity to be consumed for each type of food.

Nine to Eighteen Months

Milk and milk products:
- from a glass: whole milk until 12 months and semi-skimmed after, if desired
- plain yogurt or fruit, for dessert

- cottage cheese or mild cheese, in certain dishes

Recommended quantity:
20 oz. (625 ml) of milk per day
(4 oz. (125 ml) of yogurt or ¾ oz. (22 g) mild cheese can replace 4 oz. (125 ml) of milk)

Fruit and vegetables:
- cooked and mashed with a fork, except for ripe banana which can be eaten as is
- after 12 months, peaches and melons can be served raw; fruit juice, between 3 and 4 oz. (90 to 125 ml) per day
- avoid fruit with seeds: strawberries, raspberries, gooseberries, blackberries

Recommended quantity:
Two small portions of fruit and vegetables per day

Meat, poultry and fish:
- cut in bite-size easy-to-chew pieces
- minced meat, poached fish without bones, meatloaf

Recommended quantity:
1½ oz. (45 g) per day, approximately

Whole egg:
- after 10-12 months, the child can eat about four whole eggs per week, hard-boiled, poached or scrambled.

Cereals:
- it is preferable that baby cereals be given and the type varied throughout the week
- occasionally offer porridge or semolina and serve lukewarm

Recommended quantity:
7 tablespoons (105 ml) per day
whole-wheat bread, 1 slice per day or more

Snack foods:
- bread crusts, a quarter of a peeled apple

Foods to be avoided:
- peanuts, nuts, crisps since they can choke the young child, rich desserts, pastries and sweets since they tend to diminish the child's appetite and cause tooth decay.

One-and-a-Half to Two Years

Milk and milk products:
- milk can be taken from a cup or incorporated into desserts, such as puddings, or taken in the form of yogurt, mild cheese, or cottage cheese with fruit
- whole milk, semi-skimmed, or skimmed, according to the needs of the child or doctor's orders

Recommended quantity:
20 oz. (625 ml) per day or its equivalent in milk products

Fruit and vegetables:
- cooked and finely cut, served with the greatest colour contrasts

Monday:	carrots and broccoli
Tuesday:	cauliflower and fresh cherry tomato
Wednesday:	marrow and asparagus
Thursday:	courgettes and green beans, etc.

- certain raw vegetables can exercise a baby's gums: carrot sticks, cauliflower florets
- fruit is an excellent dessert and fruit juice may be served at snack time

Recommended quantity:
Two small portions of fruit and vegetables per day

Meat, poultry and fish:
- meat cut into strips or bite-size pieces of fish, poultry or liver cut into small cubes; roasted meat cut into small pieces

Recommended quantity:
1 ½ - 2 oz. (45-60 g) per day

Whole egg:
- serve soft-boiled, poached, scrambled or beat up in egg nog

Recommended quantity:
About four per week

Cereals:
- dry, or cooked, always served with milk

Recommended quantity:
½ cup (125 ml) per day
whole-wheat bread: one or two slices per day

Foods to avoid:
- fried foods, pastries, cakes and biscuits are unnecessary in the diet of a child of this age
- never give coffee, tea or carbonated beverages to a child
- avoid hard-to-chew foods – peanuts, nuts, crisps

Two to Five Years

The basic nutritional principles remain the same – a child eats all foods. Milk is incorporated into sauces or into desserts. Yogurt and cheese also provide calcium so essential in the building of a child's teeth and bones.

Whole fruit and vegetables are offered, either cooked or raw. Portions are increased gradually as the child grows older.

Meat is cut into pieces instead of minced; crisp bacon is also appreciated.

Sweets, cakes and pastries should not be part of the preschool child's diet. This concentrated source of calories satisfies his appetite but not his nutritional requirements and interferes with his acquisition of a varied and balanced diet.

Foods to avoid:
- fried foods and hard-to-chew foods – peanuts, nuts and crisps

Around five years of age

The child particulary rejects dishes prepared in sauces or as casseroles. Retain the basic foods: milk, vegetables, fruit, meat and cereals, served plain, without sauce or camouflaging. Children of this age prefer raw vegetables to cooked ones. The choice can, nevertheless, be large: green pepper rounds, sliced tomatoes, cauliflower florets, lettuce-and-spinach salad, cole-slaw and cubed apples, carrot salad and raisins, etc. The five-year-old is influenced by attitudes in his environment and by his friends' eating habits.

Portion Size

How much meat should a two-year old be given? What is the correct serving size of fruit for a three-year-old?

It is very important to offer appropriate food portion sizes if the child's needs and appetite requirements are to be fulfilled. It is not enough simply to divide an adult portion in half.

A healthy child knows the amount of food he requires. This presupposes, however, that the child is offered healthy foods as part of his basic diet. The child given sweets and chocolates can easily lose control of his appetite, become a glutton, and end up with a stomachache.

The table which follows indicates the approximate size of food servings suitable to a preschool child's appetite. They are very small but adequate enough to satisfy the nutritional needs of a child who eats a varied diet every day.

XII-3: *Suggested Portions from One to Six Years*

Food	1 year	2-3 years	4-6 years
Milk	½ cup (125 ml)	½ to ¾ cup (125 ml-180 ml)	¾ cup (180 ml)
Lean meat, poultry, fish	2 tablespoons (7 portions/ lb.)	3 tablespoons (6 portions/ lb.)	4 tablespoons (5 portions/ lb.)

159

Liver: once a week	2 tablespoons	3 tablespoons	4 tablespoons
Peanut butter	½ tablespoon	1 tablespoon	2 tablespoons
Egg	1	1	1
Orange juice or other juice rich in vitamin C	⅓ cup (90 ml)	½ cup (125 ml)	½ cup (125 ml)
Fruit, and yellow or green vegetables	2 tablespoons	3 tablespoons	4 tablespoons
Other vegetables (potatoes)	2 tablespoons	3 tablespoons	4 tablespoons
Other fruit	¼ cup	½ fruit	½ to 1 fruit
Bread	½ slice	1 slice	1 ½ slices
Dry cereal	⅓ cup (85 ml)	½ cup (125 ml)	½ cup (125 ml)
Cooked cereals, rice, macaroni, spaghetti	¼ cup (60 ml)	⅓ cup (85 ml)	½ cup (125 ml)

Food Preparation and Presentation

In order to stimulate a child's appetite, it is essential to offer him appetizing and easy-to-eat foods. It is very important to know why to prepare food properly so as to retain its colour, flavour, texture, and nutritional value. Limp and discoloured vegetables or dried-up and shrivelled pieces of meat will remain on a child's plate while a firm and colourful vegetable or a tender and juicy piece of meat is quickly eaten up.

Meats, Poultry, and Fish

The child enjoys these foods when they are juicy and tender, and easy to handle and chew.

The more tender cuts of meat, when gently cooked over low heat, will remain tender. The less tender cuts should be cooked longer in a small amount of liquid at a low temperature. Low heat and slow cooking will always help ensure tender and flavourful meat.

Liver, when cooked gently, maintains a good texture. Chicken livers are particularly tender and their mild flavour pleases a baby.

Meat or fish croquettes (tuna or salmon) or meatloaf, to which a larger than usual amount of liquid has been added, are popular with young children.

Poultry, which has been gently roasted (300 °F to 325 °F oven (150 °C-170 °C), 30 minutes per lb.), or simmered in a broth, produces equally tender and juicy, easy-to-chew meat, as long as it has been cut into small pieces before serving (remove small bones).

As for fish, slow-cooking over low heat preserves its fragile texture. Choose fish fillets or carefully remove all bones from fresh fish.

In all cases, lean cuts of meat and fish, fresh or frozen, should be selected. Serve in small pieces or in strips according to the child's abilities. One portion per day meets the nutritive needs of the preschool child.

Vegetables

Vegetables add colour and vitamins to the main course. The right cooking procedure will help retain these important characteristics.

Never soak vegetables in water before cooking.

Cook vegetables in a small amount of boiling, salted water. Do not wait for the vegetables to change colour or for them to become limp. Cut into small pieces or mash after cooking and serve immediately. Cooking vegetables in the pressure-cooker, or steam-cooking, also preserves their nutritive value as long as the cooking time does not exceed that indicated for each vegetable.

Retain the cooking water to cook rice or cereals in later. A blended vegetable soup supplies both milk and vegetables to the child.

When the child is able to chew, he can experiment with a

large choice of raw vegetables: carrots, green peppers, cauliflower, broccoli, turnip, celery, lettuce leaves, and cabbage.

Two small portions daily satisfy the needs of the pre-school child.

Fruit

Children like the flavour of fruit. They eat fruits cooked at the beginning, and then raw, depending on the fruit and its characteristics. Apples in particular should be peeled until the child is three or four years old to prevent choking. Note that cooked fruit compotes of apples and pears, pears and peaches, prunes and apples, or just apples are very successful.

' Serve unsweetened fruit to develop an appreciation for the real fruit flavour.

During the first two years, fruit containing small seeds, such as strawberries, raspberries, gooseberries and grapes, should not be offered.

Dried fruit (prunes, dates, figs, raisins, apricots) can be cut up into small pieces as soon as the child chews properly (after two years). Supervise the child's tooth brushing after he has eaten these fruits since they can stick to his teeth.

Every day a child must eat a vitamin-C rich fruit. Oranges and grapefruits, or their juices, fresh or frozen, are among the best sources of this vitamin. Vitaminised apple juice or tomato juice are also rich in vitamin C.

Do not choose fruit drinks or beverages instead of fruit juices. These drinks are perhaps vitamin-C enriched, but do not contain the other nutrients found in real fruit juices.

Eggs

A whole egg is added to a child's diet towards the end of the first year (ten or twelve months) and is easily accepted by the child.

Hard-boiled eggs served in an egg cup, or cut up on a

small plate and served with bread (fingers), pleases the most temperamental appetites. Poached or scrambled eggs may also be served with cottage cheese.

An older child (three to six years) likes to bite into a hard-boiled or stuffed egg. Camouflaged in egg nog or in a custard, an egg always supplies good protein to the pre-school child. A child can eat four eggs per week.

Bread and Cereals

This food group supplies protein, vitamins from the B-vitamin complex, iron and calories at a bargain price. They are part of a well-balanced diet.

The young child (three to twelve months) enjoys the taste of precooked cereals. Later, he likes cooked cereals such as porridge and semolina which have cooled, and later still, around the age of two, he crunches on dry cereals.

Advertising of dry cereals, presweetened, coloured, or puffed often makes a choice difficult when selecting these foods. But letting your children choose their own favourite cereal, is a type of freedom which can ruin a child's healthy eating habits. Whole-grain cereals *must* be selected since they retain all their nutritive qualities.

Some whole-grain cereals:
- hulled barley
- cracked wheat or bulgur
- muesli

Cooked cereals:
- porridge
- semolina
- wheat germ cereals
- brown rice
- buckwheat
- millet

Dry cereals:
- Weetabix

- Shredded Wheat (regular)
- Shredded Wheat (mini-wheats)
- Shreddies (presweetened)

A quarter cup (60 ml) of cooked cereal is equivalent to half a cup (125 ml) of dry cereal, or half a slice of whole-wheat bread.

A child with a small appetite is nourished more quickly when served cooked cereals. Always serve milk with cereal in order to reap the maximum nutritive benefits. The nutritive value of cooked cereals can be increased by replacing the water used in cooking by milk or by adding powdered milk to the cereal before cooking.

They can be naturally sweetened with dry fruit (raisins or prunes) or with fresh fruit (one-half a banana or small seasonal fruits). Add little or no sugar.

Pasta is part of this food group. It supplies less nutrients than cereal or bread. Combined with cheese, milk, eggs, meat, or vegetables, it provides variety to a meal and supplies energy.

Milk and Milk Products

This last-but-not-least important food group plays a primary role in the growth of the child. Few foods possess comparable nutritional qualities.

By the time the baby is six months old, he can start drinking whole milk. Skimmed and semi-skimmed milk is not recommended for children before the ages of twelve to eighteen months because of its high protein concentration and low caloric value. Between one to six years of age, the child must receive the equivalent of two-and-a-half cups (625 ml) of milk daily. If it is not all taken in liquid form, water or fruit juices must be provided to quench a child's thirst. Carbonated beverages or sweetened fruit drinks are to be avoided.

A child prefers milk at room temperature, which means that milk should be removed from the refrigerator some time before mealtime.

Around six months, he begins to drink from *a cup with a spout* which facilitates the transition from bottle to glass. Towards the middle of the second year, a child can handle a cup well. To avoid spills, the cup is offered at the end of the meal.

Around age two, the child drinks from a glass; a small but wide glass is easier to handle than a taller but narrower one. It is not necessary to fill it to the brim.

Around age three, a child is able to pour the milk with the help of a small container or jug. He is happy to master this technique and this may encourage him to drink a bit more milk.

At this age, an occasional straw can perform miracles. In order to increase the nutritional value of the preschool child's diet, it is recommended that milk be incorporated into soups, sauces, and desserts. Other milk products can replace the liquid milk, such as mild cheeses, yogurt, ice cream, and low fat ice-cream.

- 6 oz. (180 ml) of milk (preschool child's portion)
- 1 oz. (30 g) of soft cheese
- 6 oz. (180 ml) of yogurt
- ¾ cup (180 ml) ice-cream
- ¾ cup (180 ml) low fat ice-cream

A child must not be fed ice cream exclusively as a milk substitute under the pretext that he does not drink milk. Ice cream contains more calories than milk and might lead to an overweight problem. Ideally, ice cream can serve as a substitute on special occasions. Chocolate milk is not a good substitute for milk. It contains more calories, more sugar, and promotes a bad habit.

Mealtime Atmosphere

Timetable

Regular mealtimes promote better food consumption in the preschool child; a child eats better when fed at regular intervals. If mealtime is too late, a tired child will not eat. Breakfast takes place usually half an hour after rising, the midday meal at noon, and the evening meal at six o'clock. The evening meal can be later if a snack is provided around four o'clock.

Physical comfort at mealtime

For a child to sit down at the dinner table only to find that he has his nose at table level, that the chair rocks, that his feet do not touch the floor, or that he has to eat with oversized utensils, are factors which detract from his enjoyment of eating.

An uncomfortable child usually eats less than one who is comfortable at the dinner table.

A minimum of comfort prevents many unfortunate situations:

- high chair, with foot support
- a table suited to his needs
- smaller utensils
- good bib
- small but wide unbreakable glass, half-filled
- bowl, or convex plate rather than a flat one
- a little decor stimulates appetites
- colourful tablecloth or place mats
- centrepiece, a few dried or fresh flowers
- lit candle for a special supper meal

Child's participation

Around the age of three, a child is able to help his mother and loves to feel useful. Active participation at meal-preparation time improves his attitudes towards food and can even stimulate his appetite. Rather than having to be dragged to the table, he will sit willingly, proud of his adult accomplishments such as:

- setting the table
- placing serviettes at each place setting
- pouring milk or juice into unbreakable glasses

- placing raw vegetables or biscuits on a plate (unbreakable)
- placing bread into a bread basket.

Accidents and spills are inevitable. An understanding mother accepts them calmly and continues to ask for a child's help. An opposite reaction may create a lack of self-confidence in a child.

As a child grows, the types of tasks increase as well. He learns to:

- butter bread
- stuff celery sticks
- break eggs for father's omelette
- pod peas

His self-satisfaction grows as his responsibilities multiply.

Snacks

We live in age of coffee breaks, or snacks at any time during the day. Unfortunately it is often difficult to associate snacking with nutrition. Many favourite foods at snack time supply empty calories and suppress the appetite for the important foods served at mealtime. This phenomenon also affects the eating habits of the child; continual nibbling at biscuits, sweets, and crisps stuffs the child with calories without nourishing him and prevents him from consuming foods at mealtime which are more nutritious.

A child's need for snacks

A child will eat snacks according to his individual needs. Snacks are useful to complete the child's nutritional needs, but they should not replace meals. They must help satisfy the body's requirements but not become a social need. If this fact is kept in mind, the adult can easily forgo snacks. On the other hand, the young child eats small amounts at any given time and rapidly uses up his reserves. He is unable to go long periods without eating.

The week-old baby requires small quantities of milk, six or seven times per day. His ability to consume larger and larger amounts of food develops gradually. Around the age of ten months, he eats three or four times a day. His meals are larger, and the interval between meals is longer. Between the ages of six months and six years, a normal child who eats a good breakfast around eight in the morning, can go until noon easily without problems. An afternoon snack is often necessary and does not affect the evening meal as long as it is a healthy snack.

The three-year-old to five-year-old child who gets up early, eats breakfast rapidly, and spends the morning in a nursery school, benefits from a ten o'clock snack. Experiments conducted with small children showed that fruit juice was sufficient. Fruit juices are rich in vitamins and minerals, are easily digested, do not cause allergies, and furnish quick energy in record time.

Consider the case of a child who is all wound up at mealtime and has difficulty swallowing even a half or a quarter of the food given to him. He would certainly benefit from nutritive snacks which would fill his nutritional gaps. Care must be taken, however, since this strategy carries its own risks. The child can easily get into the habit of eating between meals rather than at mealtime.

It is thus impossible to set fixed rules with regards to snacks. The following general guidelines may help a mother decide whether or not her child does or does not need a snack and help guide her as to the correct choices:

- a child who eats like a bird at mealtime, will eat even less if snacks are offered. Snacks could therefore be the cause of a lack of appetite at mealtime.

- a healthy snack offered two to two-and-a-half hours before the next meal does not affect a normal child's appetite.

- the amount given at snacktime must be controlled in order to prevent this light meal from becoming a heavy one.

- the food chosen for snacks is of prime importance. It must complete and not detract from the nutritional needs of the child.

Criteria for a 'healthy' snack

For a child, a healthy snack should:
- attract the eye and satisfy the palate. It is pleasant to look at and good to eat
- satisfy but not fill up
- supply valuable nutrients (vitamins, minerals), but not contain empty calories
- vary from day-to-day
- keep the mind and the fingers busy
- allow the child's participation in its preparation

Ideas and Recipes for Snacks

A. Snacks rich in vitamins and minerals, but poor in calories

Unsweetened fruit juices (4 to 6 oz. (124 to 180 ml)
- apple, grape, pineapple, tomato, orange, grapefruit, watermelon juices*
- apricot or prune nectar
- 'two-fruit' drink (orange and banana juice)*

*These fruit juices may also be frozen in popsicle containers, and are a popular and refreshing treat during the summer.

Fresh fruit
- apple, quartered, cut in rings, or as apple sauce
- apricots
- whole or sliced banana
- fresh cherries
- fresh coconut, cubed
- fruit 'kebabs'*

- orange or grapefruit, in segments
- seedless green grapes, in a small bunch
- melon cubes (cantaloup, honeydew, or watermelon)
- peach or pear pieces
- prunes
- ripe strawberries, blackberries, raspberries
- mandarin oranges

Dried fruit (more concentrated in calories and sugar; brush teeth well after eating)
- raisins
- figs
- dates

Raw vegetables
- avocado cubes
- green cabbage, quartered
- carrot sticks
- florets of cauliflower or raw broccoli
- celery
- celery stuffed with peanut butter or seasoned cottage cheese
- cucumber sticks or slices
- green peas in their pods
- green pepper rings
- cherry tomatoes
- turnip sticks
- courgettes slices
- vegetable 'kebabs'

B. More Nutritional Drinks (for active children, with a large appetite)

- banana milk*
- orange milk*
- 'peanut' milk*
- grape juice and lime*
- milk, ice cream, and banana* (or strawberries)
- prune-juice shake*

C. More Nutritional Snacks (for active children, with a large appetite)

- nut or fruit bread, with cheese spread,* or served plain
- cheese cubes
- cheese sticks
- fruit and cheese (apple and cheese) 'kebabs'
- wholemeal bap
- squirrel crunch*
- cheese and vegetable (celery and cheese) 'kebabs'
- plain or fruited yogurt

*Recipes on the following pages.

RECIPES

Watermelon Drink

Ingredients
Juice of half a lemon or lime
1 cup (250 ml) orange juice, fresh or frozen reconstituted
4 cups (1 kilo) of large pieces of watermelon, with seeds removed
Preparation
1. Place all ingredients into the blender and blend well.
2. Strain if necessary (if seeds have fallen into the juice).
3. Serve cold.
Yield
5 cups (1.25 l) of juice
Comments
Watermelon supplies a certain amount of vitamins A and C

'Two-Fruit' Drink

Ingredients
1 cup (250 ml) of orange juice
1 small banana or ½ cup (125 g) strawberries
Preparation
1. Place the two ingredients into the blender and mix well.
2. Serve very cold.
Yield
2 child-sized portions

Fruit 'Kebabs'

Ingredients
2 small bananas, cut into pieces
10 to 12 large strawberries
2 oranges, quartered
Preparation
1. Thread the fruit onto 4 bamboo or wooden skewers, alternating banana, strawberry, and orange sections
2. Keep in the refrigerator, if necessary.
3. Eat as soon as possible to prevent the banana from discolouring.
Yield
4 'kebabs'
Comments
Pitted prunes may be used instead of strawberries, peaches instead of oranges, or let the child concoct his own 'kebabs.'

Banana Milk

Ingredients
1 cup (250 g) ripe bananas, cut in small pieces
½ teaspoon (2 ml) vanilla
1 cup (250 ml) semi-skimmed milk
Preparation
1. Place the two bananas and the milk into the blender and mix well.
2. Add the vanilla.
3. Refrigerate and serve cold.
Yield
2 to 3 child-sized portions

Orange Milk

Ingredients
2 pints (1 litre) semi-skimmed milk
1 6¼-oz. (180 ml) container of frozen, concentrated orange juice, unsweetened
Preparation
1. Place ingredients into the blender and mix well.
2. Refrigerate and serve cold.

Yield
6 cups (1.5 l)
Comments
This drink may be kept several days in the refrigerator.

Peanut Milk

Ingredients
2 pints (1 litre) of semi-skimmed milk
6 tablespoons (85 mg) smooth peanut butter
1 tablespoon (15 mg) honey (optional)
Preparation
1. Place peanut butter into the blender.
2. Add a small amount of the milk and mix well.
3. Add remaining milk gradually, mixing constantly. Add honey. Mix well.
4. Refrigerate. Stir gently before serving.
Yield
4 cups (1 litre)

Grape Juice and Lime

Ingredients
4 oz. (125 ml) grape juice, unsweetened
1 scoop lime sherbert
Preparation
1. Put the two ingredients into the blender; blend for 30 to 40 seconds.
Yield
2 small glasses or 1 generous portion
Comments
Another version: 4 oz. (125 ml) apple juice and 1 scoop orange sherbert is equally successful with children and adults alike.

Milk, Ice Cream and Banana (or Strawberries)

Ingredients
½ pint (250 ml) semi-skimmed milk
1 scoop vanilla ice cream
1 banana, very ripe, cut into pieces

Preparation
1. Place ingredients into the blender and mix well.
2 .Serve very cold.
Yield
2 child-sized portions
Comments
A festive snack for special days! The banana may be replaced by
¼ pint (125 ml) fresh or frozen unsweetened strawberries.

Prune-Juice Shake

Ingredients
½ pint (250 ml) milk
4 cooked prunes, pitted
⅛ pint (60 ml) prune juice
Preparation
1. Place all ingredients into the blender and mix well.
2. Serve cold.
Yield
2 child-sized portions
Comments
Excellent for gently relieving constipation

Cheese Spread (on fruit, nut, or rye bread, etc.)

Ingredients .
½ lb (250 ml) cottage cheese
¼ lb (125 ml) crushed pineapple, unsweetened
Preparation
1. Place ingredients into the blender and mix well.
2. Store in refrigerator and spread on bread just before serving.
Yield
1 cup (125 ml).
Comments
¼ lb apricot, apple, or peach puree may be used in place of the
pineapple (125 ml).

Squirrel Crunch

Ingredients
1 lb (500 g) quick-cooking oatmeal

¼ lb (125 g) shredded coconut
¼ lb (125 g) finely chopped walnuts
¼ lb (125 g) wheat germ
¼ lb (125 g) sunflower seeds
3 tablespoons (40 g) honey
3 tablespoons (40 g) corn oil
¼ teaspoon (1 ml) vanilla

Preparation

1. Set oven at 350°F (180°C).
2. Mix the first five ingredients in a large bowl.
3. Heat the honey and add to dry ingredients; add oil and vanilla. Mix with wooden spoon or hands.
4. Place mixture on well-greased baking tray. Cook for 30 minutes, stirring once during cooking. Cool.
5. Store in hermetically sealed containers. Keep in a cool place.

Yield

2 lbs (1 kilo) of cereal

Comments

After cooking, raisins or chopped dates may be added. This cereal is very nourishing. Serve only a small portion (4 to 6 tablespoons – 60 to 85 g) so as not to spoil the child's appetite.

Evaluation of Eating Habits

The formation of a child's eating habits begins in the cradle and continues throughout the preschool years, from birth to six years of age, and a finicky six or seven-year-old is likely to stay this way all his life.

Good or bad habits are acquired in the family home – not at the neighbour's. From the age of six or seven years old, the family influence decreases and exterior influences play a more dominant role – school, friends, snack bars, and so on.

A child who is accustomed to eating good food will be less inclined to adopt nutritional habits which are more or less injurious to his physical development and his health. A child who has never learned proper eating habits will be more easily attracted to coffee and doughnuts for breakfast, chips and soft drinks for lunch, and pizza and chocolate milk for supper.

Before the age of six, the situation can still be corrected. The following questionnaire will enable you to evaluate the quality of your child's eating habits. Put a tick under the appropriate 'yes' or 'no' answer.

The results are calculated according to the directions shown at the end of the questionnaire.

XII-4: *Evaluation of a Child's Eating Habits*

	YES	NO
1. He eats breakfast every morning.	___	___
2. He snacks on whatever is available throughout the morning instead of eating breakfast.	___	___
3. He drinks milk at every meal or consumes an equivalent milk substitute (see: 'Food choices at different ages' in this chapter).	___	___
4. He only drinks fruit-flavoured 'drinks' or carbonated beverages.	___	___
5. He refuses all vegetables.	___	___
6. He enjoys cooked and raw vegetables and eats them at every meal.	___	___
7. He drinks orange juice every day or eats another food rich in		

vitamin C (see:
previous chapter:
'Vitamin C').   _____   _____

8. He recognizes and
   likes whole-grain
   cereals. He eats them
   every day.   _____   _____

9. He systematically
   refuses to try new
   foods.   _____   _____

10. He eats fruits as long as
    they have been
    sweetened.   _____   _____

11. He eats liver at least
    once a week or some
    other food rich in
    iron.   _____   _____

12. He recognizes and
    likes, beef, lamb, pork
    and poultry.   _____   _____

13. He has never tasted
    fish.   _____   _____

14. enjoys mealtime.   _____   _____

15. For snacks, he eats
    biscuits or sweets.   _____   _____

16. He can control his
    appetite and knows
    when to stop eating.   _____   _____

17. He recognizes and
    likes at least three
    varieties of fish.   _____   _____

How to Calculate Your Score

- Score ten points for each 'yes' answer to questions 1, 3, 6, 7, 8, 11, 12, 14, 16, 17.
- Deduct ten points for each 'yes' answer to questions 2, 4.
- No points are awarded for any of the other 'yes' answers.

Points Obtained	Quality of Eating Habits
100	Excellent
80-100	Good
60-80	Acceptable
40-60	Improvement is desirable
0-40	It's time to do something about it!

CHAPTER THIRTEEN

The Transitional Diet – Nine to Eighteen Months

THE TRANSITIONAL DIET corresponds to a form of feeding which is adapted to the physiological and physical capabilities of the nine to eighteen-month-old child. It is called 'transitional,' since the texture of the food is more solid than purees eaten prior to this period, but softer than the foods eaten after this period. The flavours of the foods are also milder, less spicy, and less-seasoned than what will normally be served once the child is eighteen months old.

Vegetables are cooked the same way as described in the recipes for purees, then mashed with a fork after cooking. Meats, poultry, and fish are not blended for as long, or are simply minced, or cut into small pieces according to a baby's feeding skill. Fruit can be served pureed or cooked, mashed with a fork, or offered in stewed form. Some raw fruits are introduced at this time such as melon and ripe pears. Bread can be served toasted, plain, cut in strips or fingers, or as rolls as well. Rusks are also popular.

The child's appetite gradually decreases after the age of one year since the rapid-growth period is over. For this reason, suggested portions are quite small, but they take into account the nutritional needs of a child of this age.

XIII-1: *Suggested Portions from Nine to Eighteen Months*

Baby cereals:	7 tablespoons (105 ml) mixed with about $\frac{3}{4}$ cup (180 ml) milk

Fruit juice:	3 to 4 oz. (90 to 125 ml)
Vegetables and meat dinners:	¼ cup (60 ml)
Fish:	1½ oz. (45 grams)
Vegetables:	2 tablespoons (30 ml)
Stewed fruit:	¼ cup (60 ml)
Whole-wheat bread or roll	½ slice (occasionally 1 whole slice for vegetarians)
Vegetable soup:	3 oz. (90 ml)
Whole milk:	4 oz. (125 ml)
Cottage cheese:	¼ cup (60 ml)
Cheese cubes:	1 oz. (30 gm)
Yogurt:	3 oz. (90 ml)
Jellied fruit dessert:	¼ cup (60 ml)

Feeding Schedule

- a child of this age adopts the family's timetable and eats three meals a day and one snack
- he drinks from a cup, eats some foods with his fingers
- on certain days he wants to be fed, at other times he chooses to feed himself
- around twelve months of age, he starts to use a spoon
- at this age there is no room in the child's diet for rich desserts, pastries, and sweets
- avoid hard-to-chew foods, peanuts, nuts and crisps

SEVEN MEAT AND SEVEN VEGETARIAN MENUS

Transitional Menus

With Meat

1. orange juice
   barley baby cereal with milk
   whole milk

   beef, rice, and vegetables*
   apple sauce*
   whole-wheat bread
   whole milk

Vegetarian

1. orange juice
   barley baby cereal with milk
   whole milk

   rice, vegetables, and cheese*
   apple sauce*
   whole-wheat bread
   whole milk

soft-boiled egg
bread fingers
¼ peach cut in small pieces
whole milk
snack: whole milk

soft-boiled egg
bread fingers
¼ peach cut in small pieces
whole milk
snack: whole milk

2. apple juice
   oatmeal baby cereal with milk
   whole milk
   poached fish in milk*
   pureed potato and carrot
   whole-wheat bread
   ¼ ripe banana, mashed
   whole milk
   cottage cheese
   pureed prunes and apples*
   whole-wheat bread
   whole milk
   snack: whole milk

2. apple juice
   oatmeal baby cereal with milk
   whole milk
   pureed vegetables and pulses
   whole-wheat bread
   ¼ ripe banana, mashed
   whole milk
   cottage cheese
   pureed prunes and apples*
   whole-wheat bread
   whole milk
   snack: whole milk

3. orange juice
   mixed baby cereal with milk
   whole milk
   chicken with rice and vegetables*
   whole-wheat bread
   ¼ pear, mashed
   whole milk
   vegetable potage
   bread fingers
   small cube of cheese
   ¼ ripe banana, mashed
   whole milk

3. orange juice
   mixed baby cereal with milk
   whole milk
   lentils, rice, and vegetables*
   whole-wheat bread
   ¼ pear, mashed
   whole milk
   vegetable potage
   bread fingers
   small cube of cheese
   ¼ banana, mashed
   whole milk

4. apple juice
   oatmeal baby cereal with milk
   whole milk
   surprise liver and beef loaf*

4. apple juice
   oatmeal baby cereal with milk
   whole milk
   pulse surprise*

mashed courgettes
whole-wheat bread
melon in small pieces
whole milk

snack: whole milk

two-cheese macaroni*
pureed apricots
whole milk

snack: whole milk

5. orange juice
   soya baby cereal with milk
   whole milk

   pureed pork and leeks*
   whole-wheat bread
   apple sauce
   whole milk

   poached egg
   asparagus in small pieces
   ½ slice whole-wheat bread
   jellied fruit dessert*
   whole milk

   snack: whole milk

6. apple juice
   rice baby cereal with milk
   whole milk

   chicken and rice
   green beans in small pieces
   pureed apples and pears*
   whole milk

   cream of carrots*
   (see cream of vegetable soup)
   wholemeal bap
   peach yogurt
   whole milk

   snack: whole milk

7. orange juice
   soya baby cereal with milk
   whole milk

mashed courgettes
whole-wheat bread
melon in small pieces
whole milk

snack: whole milk

two-cheese macaroni*
pureed apricots
whole milk

snack: whole milk

5. orange juice
   soya baby cereal with milk
   whole milk

   vegetables au gratin*
   whole-wheat bread
   apple sauce
   whole milk

   poached egg
   asparagus in small pieces
   ½ slice whole-wheat bread
   jellied fruit dessert*
   whole milk

   snack: whole milk

6. apple juice
   rice baby cereal with milk
   whole milk

   rice and cheese
   green beans in small pieces
   pureed apples and pears*
   whole milk

   cream of carrots*
   (see cream of vegetable soup)
   wholemeal bap
   peach yogurt
   whole milk

   snack: whole milk

7. orange juice
   soya baby cereal with milk
   whole milk

poached fish*
pureed green vegetables
whole-wheat bread
puree of prune and apple*
whole milk

soft-boiled egg
cooked julienne carrots
whole-wheat bread
¼ frosty banana *
whole milk

snack: whole milk

lentils, rice, and vegetables*

whole-wheat bread
stewed apricots
whole milk

soft-boiled egg
cooked julienne carrots
whole-wheat bread
¼ frosty banana *
whole milk

snack: whole milk

*Recipes available in this book – see recipe index

XIII-2: *Nutritive Value of the 7 Transitional Menus with Meat*

Meat menus are calculated according to the suggested portions

Day	Calories	Protein (g)	Calcium (mg)	Iron (mg)	Vit.B12 (µg)	Vit. C (mg)
1	857	43	1050	18.9	4.2	70
2	822	47	733	15.7	3.2	58
3	908	49	1219	17.8	3.0	75
4	914	58	759	20.1	3.3	78
5	823	47	1049	16.9	4.0	89
6	882	38	1218	18.6	3.0	58
7	903	54	1131	18.5	3.0	75
Daily average						
	872[1]	56[2]	1022	18[3]	3.3	72[4]
Quantities Recommended:						
U.K.	800	20	600	6	no fig.	15

[1] The average number of calories is close to that recommended by the DHSS in the U.K. and represents the amount actually consumed by six to ten-month-old babies. Once more, these recommendations are considered to be quite generous, and could benefit from a

slight reduction in the recommendation for calories. For babies older then eleven months, it is easy to increase the calories simply by increasing the size of servings according to the child's appetite.

[2] In spite of the small servings of meat or fish, the entire menu supplies more than twice the quantity of required protein. Milk also contributes to the protein intake.

[3] The major source of iron comes from baby cereals. It would be difficult to satisfy an infant's requirements for iron without them.

[4] By eating a varied menu consisting of small amounts of fruit, vegetables and fruit juice, the infant easily meets his vitamin C requirements without having to resort to vitamin supplements.

XIII-3: *Nutritive Value of the 7 Vegetarian Transitional Menus*

Vegetarian menus include milk products and eggs

Day	Calories	Protein (g)	Calcium (mg)	Iron (mg)	Vit.B$_{12}$ (μg)	Vit. C (mg)
1	826	38	1107	17.6	3.7	67
2	865	42	735	16.2	3.0	56
3	908	39	1226	17.4	2.8	72
4	855	40	764	16.6	3.0	74
5	873	45	1093	17.3	4.0	93
6	902	38	1324	17.6	3.0	58
7	879	44	1104	17.5	3.0	78
Daily average						
	872[1]	40[2]	1050	17.1[3]	3.2	71
Quantities Recommended:						
U.K.	800	20	600	6	no fig.	15

[1] Despite the absence of meat, poultry, and fish, a vegetarian child can easily meet his caloric and protein requirements by eating a varied diet such as the one proposed.

A vegan child who does not eat any milk products or

eggs would benefit from a longer period of breast-feeding and foods such as tofu, baby cereals and pureed legumes added to the fruit and vegetables in order to complete his nutritional needs. A vitamin-B$_{12}$ supplement should also be taken since foods of vegetable origin do not supply this vitamin at all.

2 Protein requirements are slightly higher in the vegetarian menu in order to conform to the recommendations of the W.H.O. (F.A.O.)

3 The major source of iron comes from baby cereals. They are an important part of the young vegetarian child's diet and should not be replaced prematurely by cereals destined for the older child or adult, even if these are wholegrain cereals.

RECIPES ('Cup' refers to the American measuring cup which holds 10 fluid oz.)

Beef, Rice, and Vegetables

Ingredients
1 lb. (500 g) lean minced beef
1 teaspoon (5 g) butter or margarine
½ cup (125 g) converted rice[1]
1 cup (250 ml) vegetable cooking liquid and water
1½ cups (375 g) vegetables, finely cut. These may be either:
• ¾ cup (180 g) fresh tomatoes, peeled and chopped, plus ¾ cup (180 g) onions, green peppers, and finely chopped celery, or
• ½ cup (125 g) finely chopped celery, plus ½ cup (125 g) diced carrots, plus ½ cup (125 g) green peas, or
• ½ cup (125 g) fresh tomatoes, plus ½ cup (125 g) finely chopped celery, plus ½ cup (125 g) cut green beans or any other favourite vegetable.

Preparation
1. Bring water and cooking liquid to the boil; add rice. Lower heat and cook for approximately 10 to 15 minutes.
2. In another saucepan, fry meat gently in melted fat. Add 1½ to 2 cups (375 to 500 ml) water, half-cooked rice, and selected vegetables. Bring to the boil. Reduce heat and simmer until vegetables are tender.

3. Take from heat and cool slightly.
4. Empty into small containers $\frac{1}{4}$ cup (60 ml) and freeze.

Yield
3 cups (750 ml)
1 child-sized serving before 1 year: $\frac{1}{4}$ cup (60 ml)

Storage Life
10 to 12 weeks

1. Such as Uncle Ben's.

Rice, Vegetable and Cheese Casserole

Ingredients
$\frac{1}{2}$ cup (125 ml) white sauce, medium thickness[1]
$\frac{1}{2}$ cup (125 g) cooked rice (brown or converted)
$\frac{1}{2}$ cup (125 g) pureed vegetables (asparagus, carrots, courgettes or marrow)
6 tablespoons (90 g) grated cheddar cheese

Preparation
1. Mix all ingredients together.
2. Freeze in individual portions of $\frac{1}{4}$ cup (60 g) each or refrigerate a few days until ready to serve.
3. Heat in double-boiler or use the method described in 'two-cheese' macaroni to reheat.
4. Before serving, add 1 teaspoon (15 g) shredded cheese on top of each portion.

Yield
$1\frac{1}{2}$ cups (375 g) or 6 portions of $\frac{1}{4}$ cup (60 g)

Storage Life
3 to 4 weeks in the freezer

1. Recipe described on page 187.

Poached Fish in Milk

Ingredients
1 to 2 fillets or steaks of salt-water fish (sole, cod, plaice, haddock, salmon) – 8 oz. or 240 g

1 to 2 tablespoons (15 to 30 g) finely chopped onion
¼ to ½ cup (60 to 125 ml) whole milk

Preparation
1. Pour ¼ cup (60 ml) milk into a frying pan and heat gently. Add onion. Cook several minutes.
2. Add fish fillets or steaks. Cover and cook over low heat 5 to 10 minutes or until the fish becomes white (or light pink, as in the case of salmon), and it flakes when tested with a fork.
3. Remove from heat and flake entire fish with fork removing all bones.
4. Divide into portions (1½ oz. or 45 g) and place into small aluminium containers with a small amount of milk and onions. Cover with aluminium foil and freeze or serve one portion immediately, storing the remainder in the refrigerator for a few days.
5. Reheat in a 400°F (205°C) oven for about 10 minutes.

Yield
5 containers of portions of 1½ oz. (45 g)

Storage Life
4 to 6 weeks

White Sauce

Ingredients
2 tablespoons (30 g) butter, oil, or margarine
2 tablespoons (30 g) flour
½ cup (125 ml) whole milk
½ cup (125 ml) chicken stock or vegetable cooking liquid

Preparation
1. Melt fat in saucepan.
2. Add flour and mix well. Cook for a few minutes.
3. Gradually add liquids, stirring constantly until the sauce thickens. Cook one additional minute.
4. Cool and store in refrigerator or use immediately in a recipe.

Yield
1 cup (250 ml)

About 3 to 4 days in refrigerator
About 4 weeks in freezer

Pureed Pulses and Vegetables

Ingredients[1]
1 cup (250 g) cooked pulses (dried peas, red kidney beans, soya beans, etc.), pureed either in a blender, in a food processor or with a food mill.
½ cup (125 g) pureed green or yellow vegetables
1 cup (250 ml) white sauce, medium thickness[2] (still warm)

Preparation
1. To the warm white sauce, add pureed pulses and vegetables. Mix well.
2. Divide into portions of about ¼ cup (125 g) and empty into small aluminium containers for freezing or simply store in the refrigerator for a few days.
3. Reheat in double-boiler at serving time.

Yield
2½ cups (625 g) or 10 portions of ¼ cup (60 g)

Storage Life
4 to 6 weeks

1. Ingredients may be divided by half or by thirds so that smaller quantities can be produced.
2. Recipe described on page 187.

Chicken with Rice and Vegetables

Ingredients
½ chicken, 2-3 lb. (1 to 1.3 kg) cut into three or four pieces
1 teaspoon (5 g) finely chopped parsley
Water
2 tablespoons (30 g) minced onion
3 carrots, peeled and cut into slices
1 stalk of celery cut in pieces
1 cup (250 g) green peas or green beans, fresh or frozen.
½ to ⅔ cup (125 to 170 g) converted rice, uncooked

188

Preparation
1. Place chicken and parsley in saucepan. Bring to the boil, reduce heat, and simmer 15 minutes.
2. Add celery, onion and carrots and simmer 10 minutes longer.
3. Add the cup of green vegetables, fresh or frozen, and rice, and cook an additional 30 minutes or until all ingredients are tender.
4. Remove from heat. Take out chicken and debone carefully.
5. Place half the chicken and ½ cup (125 ml) of the cooking liquid into the blender. Blend and empty into a large bowl; blend the rest of the chicken in the same way.
6. Place the rice and vegetables and 1½ cups (375 ml) of the stock into the blender; blend and empty into a large bowl; stir the mixture, empty into containers and freeze.

Yield
About 3 cups (750 g) or 12 portions of ¼-cup (60 g) each

Storage Life
10 to 12 weeks

Comments
This preparation can be made without a blender when the child is able to chew on regular food.

Lentils, Rice, and Vegetables

Ingredients
½ cup (125 g) cooked lentils, mashed or pureed[1]
¼ cup (60 g) brown rice, cooked[2]
½ cup (125 ml) white sauce, medium thickness[3]
¼ cup (60 g) green or yellow vegetables, cooked and finely chopped

Preparation
1. Reheat white sauce slightly.
2. Add lentils, rice and vegetables, and mix well
3. Cool and store in refrigerator or empty into small freezer containers of about ¼ cup (60 ml) for the freezer.

Yield
1½ cups (375 g) or about 6 portions of ¼-cup (60 g) each

3 to 4 weeks
2 to 3 days in refrigerator

1. Any other pulse may replace lentils.
2. A white converted rice may replace the brown rice, if preferred.
3. Recipe described on page 187.

Cream of Vegetable Soup

Ingredients
½ cup (125 ml) milk
¼ to ½ cup (60 to 125 g) raw vegetables (carrot slices or cauliflower florets, asparagus or green string beans cut in pieces)
½ slice of whole-meal bread
1 teaspoon (5 g) butter or margarine

Preparation
1. Cook vegetables in small amount of water.
2. Place cooked vegetables, cooking liquid, milk, bread and butter into the blender.
3. Blend for about 30 seconds.
4. Reheat and serve.

Yield
1½ cups (375 ml) or 4 3-oz. (90 g) portions

Storage Life
1 month

Comments
These cream soups supply the child with two important foods at the same time: milk products and vegetables. They can be accompanied with a mild cheese and rusks.

Surprise Liver and Beef Loaf

Ingredients
1 lb. (500 g) chicken livers (or ox or lamb's)
1 medium onion, quartered

1¼ lb. (626 g) lean minced beef
⅔ cup (170 g) uncooked oatmeal (rapid-cooking)
1 cup (250 ml) tomato juice
1 egg
½ teaspoon salt (after age one)

Preparation
1. Preheat oven to 350°F (180°C).
2. Place the well-cleaned, raw liver, and the onion, quartered, into the blender. Blend until a smooth puree is obtained.
3. In a large bowl soak the oatmeal in tomato juice for about 10 minutes; add the puree of liver, minced meat, egg and salt, and mix well.
4. Empty into a well-greased loaf tin. Cook 60 to 75 minutes.
5. Remove from heat and leave for 5 minutes before slicing. Cut into small pieces for babies between 6 and 18 months or slice for older children.

Yield
16 servings or more for children 6 to 18 months
8 to 10 servings for children between 3 and 6 years

Storage Life
10 to 12 weeks in freezer
3 days in refrigerator

Pulse Surprise

Ingredients
1 cup (250 g) cooked white or red kidney beans
2 teaspoons (10 ml) corn oil
3 tablespoons (45 g) minced onion
¼ cup (60 g) sweet corn (pureed, if baby is not able to chew)
1 teaspoon (5 ml) tomato paste
1 tablespoon (15 ml) water

Preparation
1. Puree cooked pulses in a blender or food processor.
2. Mix water and tomato paste together.
3. Fry onion in oil. Add pureed pulses, diluted tomato paste, and sweet corn.
4. Cook over low heat until well mixed and hot.

5. Serve immediately if desired or store in refrigerator for several days.
6. This preparation can also be frozen in small freezer containers and reheated at the last minute.

Yield
Approximately 1 cup (250 ml) or 4 portions of ¼-cup (60 ml) each

Storage Life
2 to 3 days in the refrigerator
4 to 6 weeks in the freezer

Two-Cheese Macaroni

Ingredients
2 cups (500 g) cooked macaroni, blended with ¾ cup (180 ml) milk
2 eggs
1 cup (250 ml) milk
1 cup (250 g) cottage cheese
4 to 6 tablespoons (60 to 90 g) grated cheese (parmesan, cheddar)
2 teaspoons (10 g) butter or margarine
½ teaspoon salt (after age one)

Preparation
1. Beat eggs in blender; add milk, cottage cheese, grated cheese, salt, and the butter or margarine.
2. Add cooked blended macaroni. Mix well.
3. Place mixture in small individual aluminium containers. Cover with aluminium foil. Label and freeze.
4. To serve, remove from freezer and cook in 350°F (180°C) oven for about 40 minutes.

Yield
3 cups or 12 ¼-cup (60 g) portions

Storage Life
4 to 6 weeks

Comments
This macaroni contains less calories than the conventional dish since cottage cheese is used and it has a milder flavour. It can be cooked immediately after preparation in a 350°F (180°C) oven, for 30 minutes.

192

Pureed Pork and Leeks

Ingredients
5 to 6 oz. (150 to 180 g) cooked roast pork, fat removed
1 large leek
½ cup (125 ml) cooking liquid from vegetables

Preparation
1. Cook the leek. Save the green part for soups and use only the white part in this recipe.
2. Cut pork into small pieces, cut up leek, and add to blender along with vegetable cooking liquid. Blend.
3. Empty into freezer tray and freeze.

Yield
8 to 10 cubes: 1 serving represents ¼ cup (60 g)

Storage Life
10 to 12 weeks

Comments
Any lean cooked meat plus one cup of vegetables and vitamin-rich vegetable juice can constitute a similar meal.

Vegetables au Gratin[1]

Ingredients
1 cup (250 ml) white sauce, medium thickness[2]
1 cup (250 g) cooked carrots, mashed or pureed
1 cup (250 g) green vegetable, pureed (broccoli, green peas, asparagus)
6 tablespoons grated mozzarella cheese

Preparation
1. Gently reheat white sauce. Add cheese and let it melt by stirring a few minutes.
2. Add vegetables and mix well.
3. Cook and pour into small freezer containers and refrigerate until ready to serve.
4. Reheat in a double-boiler before serving.

Yield
3 cups (750 g) or 12 ¼-cup (60 g) portions

2 to 3 days in the refrigerator
4 to 6 weeks in the freezer.

1. All quantities may be decreased if a smaller quantity is preferred
2. Consult white sauce recipe on page 187.

Jellied Fruit Dessert

Ingredients
1 packet of unflavoured gelatine
¼ cup (60 ml) cold water
½ cup (125 ml) boiling water
8 oz. (250 ml) juice
8 oz. (250 ml) fruit puree (optional)

Preparation
1. Pour cold water into a medium bowl. Sprinkle gelatine over water and allow to soak.
2. Add boiling water and dissolve gelatine.
3. Add fruit juice, mixing well.
4. Add pureed fruit and mix well.
5. Pour into small individual bowls, if desired.
6. Refrigerate for a few hours and serve when gelatine is firm.

Yield
11 2-oz. (30 ml) portions

Suggestions
• unsweetened grape juice with pureed pears
• apple juice with pureed peaches or pureed banana
• frozen, diluted orange juice with pureed, frozen, sieved strawberries

NOTE: For purees, any unsweetened, canned-in-its-own-juice fruit may be used, except pineapple, which prevents the gelatine from setting.

CHAPTER FOURTEEN

The Preschool Child's Menu – Eighteen Months to Six Years

AROUND THE AGE of eighteen months, a child is usually ready to eat the same foods as other members of the family. His particular needs must not be forgotten, however: simple foods, easy-to-eat, served lukewarm or at room temperature, in small portions.

The eighteen-month-old child does not have a big appetite; his growth has slowed down. To perk up his interest in healthy foods, imagination and ingenuity must be used:

- Give your dishes amusing names: Peter Rabbit Salad, Crunchy Roll, Mystery Soufflé, Pink Surprise.

- Make the food look as attractive as possible: animal-shaped sandwiches, fruit salads arranged in the form of funny faces, a nest of vegetables; use colour and texture contrast.

- Keep mealtime a happy time. As mentioned previously, the atmosphere which prevails at the dinner table can stimulate a child's appetite or make it disappear.

- Vary the setting occasionally. Picnics in the park, on the balcony, or in the garden can help stimulate the appetite.

- Invite a friend to lunch: company stimulates appetites. All of these suggestions are applicable to a child up to the age of six.

Seven Menus

1. *Breakfast*
Grapefruit cut in sections
Crunchy Rolls
6 oz. (180 ml) milk

Lunch
Little Red Hen Salad*
Slice of bread
Pink Surprise*
6 oz. (180 ml) milk

Dinner
Small bacon omelette
Peas
Rusk or toast, cut into
triangles
Peach Ambrosia*
6 oz. (180 ml) milk

2. *Breakfast*
Orange juice
Golden Soufflé*
6 oz. (180 ml) milk

Lunch
Homemade fishfingers*
Nest of mashed potato
filled with sliced carrots,
and sprinkled with
parsley
Apple sauce
6 oz. (180 ml) milk

Dinner
Super-Duper*
Rusk with cubes of mild
cheese
Melon balls and seedless
grapes
6 oz. (180 ml) milk

3. *Breakfast*
Magic Breakfast*
Slice of toast or a roll

Lunch
Mother Hubbard Soufflé*
Grated cabbage salad
Funny Banana Bread*
6 oz. (180 ml) milk

Dinner
Meat-Loaf Surprise*
Scrumptious courgettes*
Happy Apple*
6 oz. (180 ml) milk

4. *Breakfast*
Orange cut in sections
Oatmeal and dried fruit
6 oz. (180 ml) milk

Lunch
Chicken-and-egg
casserole*
Cherry tomatoes
Slice of bread
Homemade yogurt* and
fruit in season
6 oz. (180 ml) milk

Dinner
Thin slice of ham on
buttered bread, cut into
strips
Sailboat Salad*
Frosty Banana*
6 oz. (180 ml) milk

5. *Breakfast*
Fruit Velvet*
Hot roll or bap

Lunch
Tuna Delight with
Cucumber Super-Sauce*
Peter Rabbit Salad*
Apple Snow*
6 oz. (180 ml) milk

Dinner
Small croquette of minced
beef
Nest of mashed potato
filled with finely chopped
green beans
Slice of bread
Chinese Pears*
6 oz. (180 ml) milk

6. *Breakfast*
Wake-Up Breakfast*
Slice of toast or a roll
6 oz. (180 ml) milk

Lunch
Hide and Seek (with
chicken livers)*
Broccoli florets and carrot
slices
Mashed potato
Sunshine Fruit*
6 oz. (180 ml) milk

Dinner
Macaroni cheese
Fairy Salad*
Super-Strawberry*
6 oz. (180 ml) milk

7. *Breakfast*
Vitamin-enriched apple
juice
Boiled egg
Whole meal bap
6 oz. (180 ml) milk

Lunch
Little Red Riding Hood
Special (quartered
tomatoes and celery
sticks)
Salmon Mousse
Fruit lollies*
6 oz. (180 ml) milk

Dinner
Chicken in sauce, in a nest
of rice sprinkled with
parsley
Marrow, cut into cubes
6 oz. (180 ml) milk
Bamboula Mousse*

*Recipes available in book, consult index.

RECIPES

Crunchy Roll

Ingredients
1 whole meal bap
$\frac{1}{4}$ cup (30 g) of grated cheddar cheese

Preparation
1. Cut bap in half horizontally and sprinkle each half with
   cheese.

2. Place the halves under the grill for a few minutes, until cheese has melted.

Yield
2 small portions

Little Red Hen Salad

Ingredients
½ cup (60 g) grated carrots
1½ oz. (45 g) cooked chicken, cut into cubes
2 tablespoons finely-chopped celery or green pepper
1 to 2 tablespoons (15-30 ml) mayonnaise

Preparation
1. Gently mix all the ingredients together.
2. Arrange them in the shape of a nest on the plate.
3. Garnish with a sprig of parsley.

Yield
1 portion

Pink Surprise

Ingredients
4 oz. (125 ml) plain yogurt
¼ cup (60 ml) crushed strawberries, unsweetened
1 teaspoon (5 ml) honey (optional)

Preparation
Mix the ingredients together, and serve

Yield
1 portion

Peach Ambrosia

Ingredients
3 peaches, peeled and cut into small pieces
1 sliced banana
1 tablespoon (15 ml) lemon juice
1 tablespoon (15 g) light brown sugar
¼ cup (30 g) grated coconut

Preparation
1. Cut the pieces of peach and banana onto a dessert plate.
2. Sprinkle them with the lemon juice, then sift on the brown sugar and grated coconut.
3. Serve cold.

Yield
4 small portions

Golden Soufflé

Ingredients
12 eggs
1 lb. (500 g) creamed cottage cheese
6 slices of whole-meal bread
Maple syrup or honey

Preparation
1. Heat the oven to 350 °F (180 °C).
2. Put the eggs and the cottage cheese in the blender and blend to a smooth consistency.
3. Arrange the slices of bread in a well-greased ovenproof dish.
4. Pour the egg and cheese mixture over the bread and bake for 30 minutes, or until the eggs are firm and golden.
5. Serve with maple syrup or honey.

Yield
6 adult portions, or 12 child-sized portions

Remarks
This recipe can very easily be reduced to half or a third of the quantities given above. Use a smaller baking-dish. Golden Soufflé makes an excellent breakfast on Saturdays or Sundays. If served for lunch or dinner, it provides the child with a light nourishing meal.

Homemade Fish Fingers

Ingredients
1 lb. (500 g) filleted white fish (cod, sole, haddock)
½ cup (10 tablespoons) toasted wheat germ

¼ cup (5 tablespoons) sesame seeds
1 teaspoon salt
½ teaspoon paprika
2 small eggs
2 tablespoons (30 ml) corn oil

Preparation
1. Grease a baking tray or other shallow oven-proof dish. Heat the oven to 350 °F (180 °C).
2. Place the fish fillets on a chopping-board and cut them into sticks 1 in. (2.5 cm) wide by 4 in. (10 cm) long.
3. Mix the wheat germ, sesame seeds, salt and paprika in a bowl.
4. Beat the eggs in another bowl, pour in the corn oil and whisk with a fork.
5. Roll each piece of fish in the wheat germ mixture, then soak it in the egg mixture. Roll it once more in the wheat germ mixture, then place it on the greased tray.
6. Cook in the oven for about 15 minutes.
7. Serve hot with homemade sauce tartare, a green salad and purée baked potatoes.

Yield
4 adult portions or 8 child-sized portions

Remarks
This recipe is very popular with children. It is a good way of giving them fish with all its nutritive qualities intact.
The wheat germ and the sesame seeds may be replaced with whole wheat cereals, well crushed.

Super-Duper

Ingredients
1 lb. (500 g) small courgettes (3 or 4), washed and sliced
1 cup (250 ml) homemade chicken stock
1 teaspoon salt
⅛ teaspoon basil (a pinch)
⅛ teaspoon thyme (a pinch)
½ teaspoon marjoram (a pinch)
2 cups (500 ml) milk

Preparation
1. Bring the chicken stock and salt to the boil in a saucepan, then add the courgettes, cover the saucepan and simmer until the

courgettes slices are soft (about 5 to 10 minutes).
2. Let the mixture cool a little, then add the basil, thyme and marjoram.
3. Put everything in the blender and reduce to puree.
4. Pour the puree back into the saucepan and add the milk gradually; reheat, but do not bring to the boil.
5. Serve in soup bowls, with a spoonful of plain yogurt on top if desired.

Yield
6 child-sized portions

Magic Breakfast

Ingredients
1 egg
4 oz. (125 ml) orange juice (either fresh, or frozen juice reconstituted)
2 oz. (60 ml) milk

Preparation
1. Put all the ingredients into the blender and mix for about 30 seconds.
2. Serve.

Yield
1 portion

Remarks
This breakfast is quickly prepared – and quickly gobbled up!

Mother Hubbard Soufflé

Ingredients
1 cup grated cheese – about 4 oz. (120 g)
2 tablespoons butter
4 tablespoons flour
¼ teaspoon dry mustard
½ 6-oz. (180 g) can of tuna, well drained
5 egg yolks
1 cup (250 ml) hot milk
5 egg whites

Preparation
1. Preheat the oven to 375°F (190°C).
2. Place first 7 ingredients into the blender. Blend 15 seconds.
3. Pour mixture into saucepan and cook over low heat until thick and smooth.
4. Beat egg whites until firm, but not dry, then gently fold into first mixture.
5. Pour into well-greased 3 pint (1½ litre) mould. Bake in oven about 30 minutes.

Yield
4 child-sized portions

Comments
This super soufflé never fails – children love its soft texture.

Funny Banana Bread

Ingredients
1½ cups (6 oz, 170 g) whole-meal flour
2 teaspoons baking powder
½ teaspoon baking soda
½ teaspoon salt
1 cup (20 tablespoons) natural bran
¼ cup (5 tablespoons) walnuts, chopped
¼ cup (5 tablespoons) sunflower seeds
1 egg, slightly beaten
¼ cup (5 tablespoons) honey
¼ cup (60 ml) corn oil
¼ cup (60 ml) skimmed milk
3 to 4 ripe bananas, mashed

Preparation
1. Mix first four dry ingredients together; add bran, nuts, and sunflower seeds.
2. In another bowl, mix beaten egg, oil, milk, and bananas in the blender or food processor until a smooth mixture is obtained.
3. Add this last mixture to dry ingredients and mix well.
4. Pour into oiled bread tin.
5. Cook in 350°F (175°C) oven for about 1 hour.

Yield
1 loaf

Freezer Storage Life
1 month

Comment
It is simply delicious and I suggest that the recipe be doubled so that reserves are available! Thick slices may be individually frozen and thawed in desired amounts.

Scrumptious Courgettes

Ingredients
2 lb. (1 kg) courgettes
1 8-oz.-can (240 g) tomato sauce
2 oz (60 g) grated cheese
salt, pepper, and oregano

Preparation
1. Preheat oven to 350 °F (180 °C), and grease an oven-proof dish.
2. Wash courgettes, and cut into thin slices; do not peel.
3. Place a layer of courgettes into dish and season with salt and pepper; place a second layer, and season again.
4. Mix the tomato sauce and oregano, and pour over courgettes
5. Sprinkle with cheese and cover dish.
6. Cook about 25 minutes.

Yield
6 portions

Freezer Storage Life
3 months

Happy Apple

Ingredients
4 apples
4 teaspoons (20 g) honey
4 tablespoons (60 g) grated coconut
Lemon juice

Preparation
1. Heat the oven to 350 °F (180 °C).
2. Core the apples and cut them in two.

3. Put them in an oven-proof dish or on a sheet of aluminium foil, sprinkle each half with honey and coconut, then sprinkle with lemon juice.
4. Cover the dish, wrap it in aluminium foil.
5. Bake in the oven for 20 to 30 minutes.

Yield
4 portions or 8 half portions

Chicken and Egg Casserole

Ingredients
¾ slice whole meal bread, crumbled
¼ cup (60 ml) milk
12 oz (340 g) chicken, cooked and diced
1 tablespoon chopped onion
¼ teaspoon salt
1 tablespoon chopped parsley
2 tablespoons (30 ml) corn oil
1 egg + 1 egg yolk

Preparation
1. Heat the oven to 350 °F (180 °C).
2. Soak the bread in the milk, then add the chicken, onion, salt, parsley and oil.
3. Beat the egg yolks and add them to the mixture.
4. Beat the egg white until stiff, then fold it carefully into the mixture.
5. Pour the mixture into an oven-proof dish, and stand this in a cake tin with hot water in it.
6. Cook for about 30 minutes, or until the centre of the mixture has set. Then remove the dish from the oven, and serve.

Yield
4 portions

Homemade Yogurt

Ingredients
5 cups (1.2 litre) semi-skimmed milk
¼ cup (5 tablespoons) powdered skimmed milk
¼ cup (60 ml) plain yogurt

Preparation
1. Mix milk and the milk powder together.
2. Heat mixture to boiling (180 °F – 82 °C); check with thermometer.
3. Remove mixture from heat and cool to 113° to 116 °F (46 °C) (This will take about 20 minutes).
4. Place yogurt into a large pyrex or earthenware bowl. Gradually add milk and mix well.
5. Cover bowl with cling film or aluminium foil; (wrap bath towel around it to keep heat in and shield it from draughts).
6. Place bowl in a warm place where the temperature does not go above 150 °F (65 °C); (a warm oven with heat turned off and checked with thermometer, near a radiator, or in a warm room where there are no draughts).
7. Let mixture set for 5 to 12 hours. Do not disturb bowl. The warmer the place, the quicker the yogurt will form. In a cooling oven, it will take about 8 to 10 hours – or overnight. As soon as the yogurt has set, refrigerate immediately. Use this yogurt in the preparation of recipes which follow.

Comments
Yogurt preparation is simple but delicate. Temperature must be kept properly maintained to guarantee success.

Yield
5 cups (1.2 l)

Storage life
1 month

Sailboat Salad

Ingredients
1 small cantaloup melon
2 slices of packaged Swiss or cheddar cheese
Lettuce, washed, well drained, cut into strips
4 toothpicks

Preparation
1. Place lettuce in the bottom of 4 bowls.
2. Quarter melon, remove seeds, and place each quarter on a bed of lettuce.

3. Cut cheese slices diagonally, then use toothpicks as 'masts' to hold the triangles of cheese (the 'sails') and stick them into the cantaloup quarters.
4. Serve with cold meats.

Yield
4 portions

Frosty Banana

Ingredients
1 peeled banana
2 tablespoons (30 ml) plain yogurt
2 tablespoons grated coconut or finely chopped nuts

Preparation
1. Cover banana with yogurt.
2. Roll in coconut or chopped nuts.
3. Place 'frosty' banana on a dessert plate and serve.

Yield
1 portion

Fruit Velvet

Ingredients
1 cup (240 ml) plain yogurt
4 oz. (125 ml) frozen grape juice or frozen orange juice

Preparation
1. Place ingredients into blender, and blend to milkshake consistency.
2. Serve.

Yield
3 4-oz. (125 ml) portions

Comments
Simply delicious.

Tuna Delight

Ingredients
1 6-oz. (180 g) can tuna
1 egg beaten
¼ cup (60 ml) milk
1 tablespoon vegetable oil
¼ cup (5 tablespoons) chopped onion
1 tablespoon finely chopped parsley
½ teaspoon basil

Preparation
1. Preheat oven to 425°F (220°C).
2. Mix together: egg, milk, oil, onion, parsley and basil.
3. Flake tuna with a fork and mix it with the other ingredients.
4. Pour mixture into a small oven-proof dish.
5. Bake in the oven for about 25 minutes.

Yield
4 child-sized portions

Freezer Storage Life
3 months

Comment
To round off this seafarer's meal, accompany with Cucumber Super-Sauce.

Cucumber Super-Sauce

Ingredients
1 small cucumber, grated, with or without peel
½ teaspoon chopped onion
¼ cup (60 ml) mayonnaise
1 tablespoon finely-chopped parsley
¼ cup (60 ml) plain yogurt
1 tablespoon (15 ml) lemon juice

Preparation
1. Throughly mix all ingredients and serve with fish.

Yield
¾ cup (180 ml)

Comment
A guaranteed winner!

Peter Rabbit Salad

Ingredients
¼ cup (30 g) grated carrot
¼ cup (30 g) grated cabbage
1 tablespoon mayonnaise

Preparation
1. Mix all ingredients together, and serve.

Yield
1 portion

Apple Snow

Ingredients
1 cup (250 ml) unsweetened apple sauce
2 egg whites
1 tablespoon honey
1 tablespoon grated lemon rind

Preparation
1. Place ingredients into the blender and beat to the consistency of whipped cream.
2. Serve in small individual bowls.

Yield
4 to 6 portions

Chinese Pears

Ingredients
4 ripe pears
2 oz. (60 g) finely chopped walnuts
4 teaspoons honey
1 teaspoon cinnamon or ginger

Preparation
1. Preheat the oven to 350 °F (180 °C).
2. Peel and core pears; place in oven-proof dish.
3. Mix together nuts and honey.
4. Stuff centres of the pears with the honey and finely chopped nuts mixture.
5. Sprinkle with cinnamon or ginger.
6. Cook for about 30 minutes, or until the pears are soft.
7. Serve either hot or warm.

Freezer Storage Life
3 to 5 months

Wake-Up Breakfast

Ingredients
1 cup (250 ml) fresh or frozen reconstituted orange juice
1 cup (250 ml) fresh strawberries or quartered peaches
2 eggs
½ cup (10 tablespoons) powdered skimmed milk
½ cup (125 ml) water

Preparation
1. Place all ingredients in the blender and blend thoroughly.
2. Serve.

Yield
4 to 6 child-sized portions

Freezer Storage Life
6 weeks

Comment
This is a complete breakfast in a glass.

Hide and Seek with Chicken Livers

Ingredients
4 slices of bacon
4 chicken livers

Preparation
1. Turn on the grill
2. Cut chicken livers and slices of bacon in half.
3. Wrap each piece of liver in a strip of bacon and secure it with a toothpick.
4. Place under the grill for about 8 minutes, or until the bacon is crisp. Turn once during cooking.
5. Remove from the heat, take out the toothpicks and serve.

Yield
4 small portions (2 pieces per portion)

Freezer Storage Life
3 months

Comment
When I saw my daughter eating her Hide and Seek with obvious relish, I said to her, 'So now you like liver, do you?' 'No, Mum,' she replied, 'it's the bacon I like.'

Sunshine Fruit

Ingredients
2 pears
2 bananas
12 unsweetened strawberries, either fresh or frozen
1 cup (250 ml) plain yogurt
1 teaspoon cinnamon
A few chopped nuts

Preparation
1. Peel and core pears; cut into pieces.
2. Peel and slice bananas.
3. Wash and dry the strawberries, and cut them in half.
4. Mix together the fruit, yogurt and cinnamon and refrigerate for at least 1 hour.
5. Sprinkle with chopped nuts and serve.

Yield
6 child-sized portions

Comment
Seedless grapes may be substituted for the strawberries.

Fairy Salad

Ingredients
1 apple, grated, with or without peel
¼ cup (30 g) raisins
1 tablespoon mayonnaise

Preparation
1. Mix together all ingredients, and refrigerate.
2. Serve on a lettuce leaf.

Super-Strawberry

Ingredients
1 envelope unflavoured gelatin
¼ cup (60 ml) cold water
¼ cup (60 ml) boiling water
1 6¼-oz. (180 ml) can frozen concentrated orange juice, unsweetened
1 6¼-oz. (180 ml) can cold water
1 cup (125 g) unsweetened fresh or thawed strawberries

Preparation
1. In large bowl sprinkle gelatin over ¼ cup (60ml) cold water, and let soak for 5 minutes.
2. Pour ¼ cup (60 ml) boiling water over gelatin mixture and mix well until gelatin has dissolved.
3. In blender, blend strawberries, undiluted orange juice concentrate, and container of cold water.
4. Blend until smooth.
5. Pour the pureed strawberry and orange mixture into gelatin mixture. Mix well.
6. Refrigerate a few hours until firm.

Yield
6 portions

Fruit lollies

Ingredients
2 cups (500 ml) plain yogurt

1 6¼-oz. (180 ml) can of fruit juice, unsweetened and undiluted
Lolly sticks and moulds

Preparation
1. Pour yogurt into a bowl. Thicken in freezer for about 1 hour.
2. Pour undiluted frozen fruit juice into blender together with
   the half-frozen yogurt, and blend until smooth.
3. Pour the mixture into lollipop moulds, push a lollipop stick
   into each mould, and freeze.
4. To serve, run very hot water over the moulds to loosen the
   lollipop.

Yield
10 fruit lollies

Comment
Try orange juice, grape juice, pineapple juice – they are all delicious, for children and adults alike.

Bamboula Mousse

Ingredients
1 cup (¼ lb – 125 g) cooked pitted prunes
3 ripe bananas
½ teaspoon almond extract
5 tablespoons grated coconut (optional)

Preparation
1. Place all ingredients into the blender, blend until smooth.
2. Mix in the grated coconut.
3. Serve

Yield
4 to 6 child-sized portions

Freezer Storage Life
3 to 5 months

CHAPTER FIFTEEN

A Few Special Problems

Whims

1. What can you do with a child who refuses to eat?

To BEGIN WITH, it is not unusual to find a preschool child on a 'hunger strike.' But what causes this behaviour? If the child simply refuses to eat at mealtime but stuffs himself between meals with foods which do not provide any nutrients, but are sufficient in calories to fill him up, by the end of the day there will be a serious lack of protein, calcium and vitamins.

If this situation persists for any length of time, the reasons must first be found in order to arrive at the solution.

Generally speaking, a refusal to eat is a behavioural problem which goes beyond the context of the meals themselves; it is a reaction to the general attitude of the child's parents. He is reacting perhaps because he was forced to finish his bottle as a baby, or was overfed during his first few years. He finds it easy to do so since he has become less hungry; he also feels the need to assert himself; he seeks attention; he realizes that his refusal to eat worries his parents so he starves himself to win attention and get his own way.

What not to do:

- force the child to remain at the table until his plate is empty

- Promise dessert if he finishes what is on his plate
- serve leftovers from the last meal on the same plate for his next meal
- make him eat 'one bite for Daddy – and one for Mummy – and one for Grandma,' and so on
- talk about the nutritional content of the food; i.e., foods which make you grow, are good for the hair, etc.

What to do:

- calmly accept food refusal
- do not show disapproval, or concern, either visibly or verbally
- if the child is hungry between meals, explain gently but firmly that the next meal is coming soon. Do not tell him that he is hungry because he missed the last meal.
- avoid speaking about food, vitamins, or food likes or dislikes at the table
- be prepared to see your child go hungry for a few days. He will acquire better eating habits as a result
- give him the extra attention he is looking for – but between meals!

2. Will the growth of a child be stunted if he refuses to drink milk?

Milk and milk products are very important during a child's growth. They play an important role in teeth and bone formation and are very difficult to replace as no other food group possesses the same nutritive qualities. The child can grow, but his bones and teeth may grow more slowly and be formed weakly.

Why does a child refust to drink milk? Is it too hot? Too cold? Is the glass too big? The following recommendations may prove helpful.

Why does a child refuse to drink milk? Is it too hot? Too cold? Is the glass too big? The following recommendations may prove helpful.

Serving Milk
Serve milk in a smaller, colourful glass...with a straw. A three-year-old child can serve himself from a small jug.

Setting an Example
The child is first and foremost an imitator. If parents drink milk at mealtime, the example they set is far more effective than verbal encouragement. If extra calories and unsaturated fats are a problem for the parents, skimmed milk can easily be chosen instead.

Camouflaging it
Should the child consistently refuse to drink milk, he might prefer to 'eat' his milk. At breakfast give him hot cereals cooked in milk. At noon, offer him yogurt or a scoop of ice cream dessert. For supper, serve his meat, poultry, or fish in a white sauce, or give him a cream of vegetable soup with cubes of mild cheddar cheese (see substitutes).

Dressing It Up
Milk goes down smoothly if its taste is disguised. Try serving milk mixed with fruit juice, or a 'superdrink' made with yogurt and fruit juice. Do not add honey, sugar, or chocolate to the milk (consult snack recipes).

3. Can vegetables be replaced in the pre-school child's diet?

Vegetables are often the problem food since mothers usually insist they be eaten. Forcing a child to finish his vegetables will probably reinforce his dislike.

Before removing them from his diet, try to find out why he dislikes them.

a) Do the parents like vegetables and eat a large variety regularly?

Where food tastes are concerned, the parents' eating patterns and their influence on the child should never be underestimated. The father's food preferences, in particular, have a great bearing on the eating habits of his children. If he dislikes broccoli, carrots, or cauliflower, his children will usually refuse to eat them too. If he enjoys eating them, the children will imitate him.

The way in which vegetables are prepared and served plays an important role in their acceptance. Overcooked, colourless vegetables without texture or taste will no doubt be rejected. A well-cooked vegetable, tender but firm, brimming with taste and colour, and served in a small quantity, is far more easily accepted.

The child who was initiated early as an infant or before the age of two to a variety of vegetable flavours wil be more likely to accept vegetables later on as well.

b) Has the mother tried all the vegetables available before giving up?

A mother should not be discouraged after one food refusal. Perseverance is the key to acquiring healthy eating habits. A vegetable which is usually refused suddenly becomes appetising when served with a favourite dish.

c) Raw vegetables are usually more popular with children.

This is an advantage because vitamins and minerals are preserved and the cellulose fibre found in vegetables is responsible for the proper functioning of the intestines. One more reason for them to be included in a child's diet – they can be eaten at mealtime or as a snack. Here are a few examples: lettuce and spinach salad, green pepper and cucumber rings, cherry tomatoes, cauliflower florets, carrot and celery sticks, and grated cabbage and carrot salad.

If a mother has tried everything and the child still persists in refusing both cooked and raw vegetables, another source of vitamins, minerals and cellulose must be found. Nature thinks of everything. Fortunately fruit possesses almost the same nutritive qualities as vegetables. The two vegetable portions a child must consume daily can temporarily be replaced by two fruit portions.

The fruit family offers many variations in colour, taste, and nutritive values. A child will benefit more if a fruit rich in vitamins and minerals is chosen. Some of the best ones are: melon, strawberries, citrus fruit (oranges and grapefruit), fresh or dried apricots, peaches, prunes, watermelon. Reconstituted frozen fruit juices (orange, grapefruit and grape) are good sources of vitamin C. Apricot and prune nectar supply also vitamin A and iron. Fruit-flavoured drinks enriched with vitamin C are not recommended.

4. If a child refuses to eat meat, can it be replaced with equally nutritious foods?

When a child systematically refuses to eat a food, I would suggest you reread the first section of this chapter.

Meat is not indispensable in the child's diet. It can be replaced by other equally good protein sources, such as poultry, fish, eggs, or cheese. However, every time you remove a food from a child's diet, you run the risk of making the diet more monotonous. One ounce (30 g) of meat can be replaced by:

- 1 oz. (30 g) fish, fresh or canned
- 1 oz. (30 g) poultry
- 1 oz. (30 g) cheese, such as cheddar
- 1 egg
- $\frac{1}{4}$ cup (60 ml) cottage cheese
- 6 oz. (180 ml) yogurt
- 6 oz. (180 ml) milk
- $\frac{1}{2}$ cup (125 ml) cooked pulses (beans, lentils, dried peas)

A child who eats neither meat nor offal (liver, heart, kidney), should be given dried peas (butter beans, kidney beans, haricot beans), dried fruits, whole-grain cereals, and green vegetables in order to obtain a sufficient amount of iron. This nutrient plays an important role in the circulation of oxygen in the blood.

5. How should you discipline a child who plays at mealtimes?

Discipline at mealtimes is no different from discipline in any other of the day's activities. It implies calm and consistent authority on the part of the parents. It does not mean strict regimentation, but rather the acceptance of certain rules.

Mealtimes should be occasions for relaxation and family conversation – but not for playing. The child who has had a rest before his meal will be less excitable at the table, and if the meal is prolonged with a lot of adult conversation, the child should be allowed to leave the table.

6. How can one reduce a child's sugar consumption?

The solution is simple: don't give him any!

The sugar in sweets, carbonated beverages, and other sweet things supplies calories which provide the child with temporary energy, but do not promote growth or keep him fit. An over-consumption of sweets interferes with a child's appetite and promotes tooth decay. Parents themselves are largely responsible for the problem; they confer all kinds of powers on sugar.

'You've been such a good boy, here's a sweet.'

'Here, have a piece of chocolate. It'll make you feel better.'

'You don't like your carrots? – Try them with a bit of sugar.'

'Isn't plain grapefruit bitter?'

'Here's a bit of sugar, now finish your cereal!'

'Sweetened orange juice is so much better!'

'A meal without a nice sweet dessert just isn't a proper meal.'

'My child only likes chocolate milk.'

These comments illustrate how parents can inculcate a taste for sugar, however unconscious it may be. Sugar has insidiously invaded our eating habits. The consumption of

90.6 lbs. (41.1 kg) yearly, per person, in Great Britain, is too much!

We must act now to instill new family eating habits, and help our children rather than punish them by eliminating sweets as a 'reward and punishment' tactic.

Will a child easily accept this change if he sees his parents eating sweets while watching television at night?

Good resolutions are made together as a family. You should:

- do away with temptation – do not buy any more sweets
- gradually decrease sweet desserts and replace them with fruits
- avoid giving sugar an emotional value (reward, consolation, pleasure, or a treat).

A young child who learns to savour and appreciate the true taste of fruit, vegetables and milk will not become a slave to sugar.

Prevention is better than cure!

7. Is it dangerous to drink too much milk?

Some children drink too much milk, and this can have some adverse effects. Milk is very nourishing, but it is not a perfect food. As mentioned previously, a vitamin D supplement has to be given as early as three weeks of age to complete the milk diet. As the child grows, milk is less and less able to supply all the essential nutrients. It is particularly deficient in iron and vitamin C.

A child who drinks too much milk, that is a good deal more than the recommended amount (20 oz. (625 ml) a day) will not be hungry. He will nibble at mealtime and will not eat the right amount of meat, vegetables, fruit or cereals, and runs the risk of becoming anaemic.

Milk is an important part of a balanced diet. However, it must work with other foods in order to fulfil its role properly. Drinking too much milk is a bad habit which can be corrected as follows:

- by decreasing milk consumption between meals and replacing it with fruit juice or even water

- by offering the glass of milk at the end of the meal rather than at the beginning.

Health Inquiries

1. The child who is allergic to milk.

Many mothers think that their child is allergic to milk, when in fact the problem lies elsewhere. Seventy-five percent of mothers are wrong in their assessment. In fact, only 0.3% to 7% of infants are allergic to milk. A baby who vomits after feeding is not allergic to milk. He has perhaps drunk too rapidly without stopping to burp. Normal feeding time is between 20 and 30 minutes.

The new born baby who suffers from cramps may temporarily exhibit an intolerance to milk, but he is not allergic to it. A mother who changes a baby's formula every few weeks without consulting her doctor is not solving the problem of milk intolerance but rather is interfering with her child's normal digestion.

A baby who is really allergic to milk can still grow normally thanks to various milk-free formulas. Soya-based formulas such as Wysoy and Cow & Gate Formula 'S' are two examples. A family physician or pediatrician is the only one qualified to diagnose a milk allergy and consequently to suggest an appropriate formula for the baby.

2. The constipated child.

A proper diet can play an important role in the treatment of chronic constipation.

Certain foods containing cellulose help normal intestinal functions: bran cereals, whole-grain cereals, raw fruit and vegetables and dried fruit (prunes, raisins, dates, figs). A child who drinks too much milk and does not consume the proper amount of fruit and vegetables may well become constipated.

Physical exercise and adequate consumption of liquids

(water and fruit juice) will also help combat constipation. The use of laxatives is not recommended since they make the intestines 'lazy.'

3. The child who suffers from diarrhoea.

Diarrhea is always a serious problem, more so in an infant than in a preschool child. In all cases, it is better to consult with the family doctor to ensure that proper treatment is received.

A child who consumes too much sugar or is over-excited, is a likely candidate for diarrhoea.

4. The child who has an upset stomach.

It is recommended that a doctor should be consulted whenever a small child (from birth to two years) suffers from indigestion.

After this age, the usual treatment is a prolonged fast ($\frac{1}{2}$ to 1 day) after vomiting has ended. This gives the tired stomach a rest.

A few sips of mineral or tap water every half-hour will quench the child's thirst. Solids are gradually introduced in the days that follow. Semi-solid foods which are easy to digest are first introduced: strained, cooked cereals; toast; soft-boiled egg; custards; ripe banana; apple sauce.

5. The child who is too thin.

As we saw in Chapter Fourteen, the one-and-a-half-year-old to six-year-old child grows erratically. Because of these growth spurts and slowdowns, the preschool child does not maintain a constant level of appetite. His appetite is capricious and he seldom has much reserve of fat especially if he is very active. When a child suddenly starts to grow rapidly he is unable to put on enough weight to balance the growth spurt in height.

This is no cause for alarm. The situation can be improved by controlling both the child's activity and his nutritional intake. By decreasing his level of activity and increasing the number of calories in his diet, he will be able to gain weight.

Up to the age of six, a child needs a certain amount of sleep to allow him to recuperate both physically and emotionally. If the thin child never rests during the day, and goes to bed at the same time as his parents at night, it is obvious that he is overexpending his energy and he is unable to build up his fat reserves.

Without imposing a daily nap on a child, it should be possible to arrange for a period of at least one hour in the day during which he can rest physically and emotionally by listening to a story, colouring, or listening to records. Bedtimes can be advanced in order to increase the child's sleep time. It should not be forgotten that a tired child has less appetite than one who is well rested. In addition, the child should probably receive more calories. A review of his eating habits is essential:

- Does the child eat at mealtime?
- Does he eat large or small quantities?
- Does he snack between meals?
- Does he like many different kinds of foods?
- How much does he eat in one day?

A precise answer to each of these questions will enable a parent to develop a plan to enrich a child's diet.

If the child is a small eater, you must bear in mind that regular mealtimes promote a better appetite, and that snacking between meals merely reduces it.

If, on the other hand, he is a big eater, you must enrich his menus in order to increase the number of calories without increasing the quantity of food he eats.

At breakfast, for example:

- cook his cereals with whole milk rather than with water
- serve him omelettes or scrambled eggs instead of soft-boiled or poached eggs
- offer him baps or rolls instead of plain toasted bread
- give him whole milk instead of semi-skimmed milk.

At other meals:

- serve milk-based or cream soups instead of stocks, consommés, or vegetable juice
- serve meat, poultry, or fish with a white or brown sauce
- serve mashed potatoes (with milk and butter) instead of plain, boiled, or baked potatoes
- dress salads with sour cream or thick dressings
- add butter to the vegetables
- give him bread, biscuits and desserts made of milk between meals, if he is still hungry
- offer him milkshakes (milk, fruit, and ice cream), etc.
- prepare biscuits made with dried fruit and nuts.

A daily walk in fresh air will also stimulate his appetite.

6. The fat child.

Before the age of six, the fat child is less common than the thin one. It is important to remedy this situation before it is too late.

In the U.K. 15% of adolescents, 26.5% of adults between 20 and 39 years of age, and 48.3% of adults between 40 and 65 years are overweight.

This is a sobering situation especially when one considers that obesity in the adult increases his chances of such illnesses as hypertension, diabetes and atherosclerosis. Concern is growing among cardiologists in Great Britain over the long-term effects of wrong diet on the health of the nation's young people. Children as young as 8 years may already be showing signs of arteries 'furred up' by excessive consumption of fatty foods.

An annual visit to the paediatrician or to the family doctor will enable parents to follow and review their child's weight curve. If he is found to be overweight it will be necessary to try and get him to lose a few pounds and change his life-style as well as his eating habits.

In fact, several studies have shown that an overweight child does not eat more than a normal weight one, but he is much less active.

223

An overweight child must first and foremost exercise more and . . .watch less television!

Establishing the cause of the overweight is as important as the dietetic treatment for it, per se. A child who eats to fulfil a need for affection will respond poorly to restrictions on his diet, whereas a child who eats a lot simply because everyone around him eats a lot, will react better.

A weight-loss diet for a child of this age will hardly be noticed if the mother plans it carefully. Calories are decreased only slightly because the high requirements for growth must be met. A loss of 1 to 2 lb. ($\frac{1}{2}$ to 1 kg) per week is sufficient.

The basic foods should never be eliminated: milk, meat, fruit, vegetables and cereals. On the other hand, lower calorie substitutes may be used, as long as nutritional quality is not sacrificed. Useless or superfluous foods, such as sweets and crisps, can always be eliminated.

A child will lose one pound ($\frac{1}{2}$ kg) per week by replacing daily:

- instead of 20 oz. (625 ml) whole milk, serve 20 oz. (625 ml) skimmed milk
- instead of a rich snack (date squares), serve a fruit (1 apple)
- instead of a rich dessert ($\frac{1}{2}$ cup or 125 ml) ice cream, serve a fruit (1 peach).

A reduction of 500 calories daily provides a painless way to lose weight.

The mother of a child who is prone to gaining weight should watch very closely the quality and the quantity of the food she serves her child. She must also be aware that the cooking method affects the number of calories in the food served. Fried foods or foods cooked in butter supply more calories than grilled or steamed foods.

Thanks to parental foresight, the overweight child who adopts a healthier life-style (better balanced diet and increased physical activity) before the age of six, is ensuring himself a happier and healthier life.

CHAPTER SIXTEEN

Knowledge Leads to Love

THE FIRST FEW years of a child's life are the years in which he explores the world around him. They are years filled with new visual, auditory, gustatory and olfactory experiences.

A child slowly discovers colours, textures, shapes, smells and tastes. After the first few months, his eyes are attracted to the red toy rather than the little beige dog, to the orange carrot, rather than green beans. His fingers react to different textures and can differentiate between a velvet doggy, a smooth ball and a rag doll. His taste buds experience a whole range of new tastes and even at this age he makes his likes and dislikes known (mashed bananas are eaten faster than pureed meats). His ears recognize the music-box's melody. His nose learns to sniff and enjoy pleasant smells.

Everything that is taken in and retained during the first years of life is accomplished through his senses. The more opportunities a child has to see, touch, taste, smell and hear, the more he gets to know the world around him and the better prepared he is to deal with it.

Senses must be exercised just as muscles must be exercised. The child grows to love the things he knows: the pretty toy he looks at, the cat he strokes, the melon he tastes, the rose he smells, the song he hears.

Food is a part of the child's world. The more opportunities he has to learn about different foods, the greater are the chances that he will like them.

Always keeping the objective of forming good eating habits in mind, this last chapter suggests activities, games, and experiences for the child which will enable him to discover a wide variety of foods while having fun.

Let's visit the supermarket
(two to two-and-a-half or older)

It is a real pleasure for a child to go to the supermarket with his mother. Sitting in a shopping trolley, he discovers a whole new world of foods.

This experience can be both pleasant for the mother and valuable for the child, even if it only takes place occasionally.

It is better to go shopping for food after having eaten. This spares the mother the wails of a hungry child. In the same vein, buying sweets or biscuits to calm the over-excited child must not be done. If it's time for his snack, a child should be given an apple, or a small packet of raisins to nibble.

During this visit, the child learns by watching his mother fill her shopping trolley. In his mind the food that his mother buys is good food: good for the family and good for him. If all he sees is canned goods, frozen foods, and prepared dishes, he will not learn very much and will get a very poor idea of what constitutes a good diet.

If, on the other hand, the mother buys basic foods (meat, fruit, and vegetables, cereals, and milk products), and she explains why she is buying such-and-such a vegetable or cut of meat (to make a salad, to prepare some casserole), he will feel he is actively participating and this will make him very happy. Every now and then he should be allowed to make the choice himself between two kinds of cheeses, two vegetables or two fruits, or fruit juice of equal nutritional value. If he has had a say in the actual choice of the food, he will be interested in getting to know it, and will hardly refuse it when it appears on his plate.

The fruit and vegetable market
(suitable for a three-year-old)

A family visit to this market at the height of the season is a treat which should be fully taken advantage of. Throughout the year it is possible to purchase fruits and vegetables in an open-air market. This is one activity a child should not miss.

He can savour the smell of fresh fruits and vegetables, and will learn to recognize the characteristics of good vegetables or fruit: the whiteness of the cauliflower, the firmness of green peppers, the shiny skin of aubergines and courgettes, the deep colours of strawberries, and so on.

What a pleasure to taste the first carrots of the season! There is no substitute for the smell of vegetables and fruits in season and this is the perfect way to give our children a taste for them.

The fish stall
(suitable for three-year-olds or older)

The fish stall presents nature's wonders to the curious and attentive child. No need to visit the sea to see cockles and mussels, winkles, prawns, lobsters, crabs, eels and a host of fish species of many shapes, sizes and colours. Get him to recognize different kinds of fish by the colours and patterns of their iridescent scales.

A child will like fish if he has acquired a taste for it while very young and if his mother prepares it so that all its flavour is retained.

To double this pleasure, let the child choose his own favourite fish once in a while.

The farm (suitable for three-year-olds and over)

To gather a still-warm, freshly laid egg in the hen house, to see a cow being milked, to discover a pig's curly tail, to run in meadows, to go to a barbecue, to pick a ripe apple – these are but a few of the experiences which teach a child about the origins of his food. Throughout the summer, many farms open their doors to welcome families interested in sharing these experiences firsthand.

A walk in the country (for three-year-olds or older).

With a pair of good sharp eyes, and a little luck, one can usually discover several edible plants growing wild during a simple walk in the country. Every month of the summer has something different to offer. From June to September you can find the oddly named 'fat-hen' growing particularly in recently disturbed soil. It should be cooked in the same way as spinach. In June, dandelion greens make an excellent salad and are rich in vitamin C. July brings wild strawberries and wild raspberries. In August, tiny delicious bilberries are available. Autumn brings various nuts – walnuts, hazel nuts, cobs and chestnuts.

A child soon learns to appreciate the flavour of these edible wild plants which he has picked for himself in the countryside. However, it is vital that you explain to a child that not all plants and berries can be eaten – some are poisonous.

Let's try planting our own vegetables

All that is needed to grow one's own vegetables is earth, water, sunshine, and a lot of tender love and care. Even in the heart of the big city, a child can still experience the joys of a vegetable garden.

Cherry tomatoes (for three-year-olds and older)

At the end of March, cherry tomato plants are available at garden centres. They can be planted in ten-inch (25 cm) diameter pots; the pots are then placed in a sunny window. The aspiring young gardener is then responsible for their care and watering. When the warm weather arrives, the pots are put outdoors on a terrace or balcony in a sunny spot. The plants must be staked, watered regularly and protected against pests like green fly and white fly. If the young gardener has done his job well, he can proudly harvest and eat several miniature tomatoes.

Little beans grow into big beans (for three-year-olds or older)

By sowing beans, the child is able to observe every step in the development of a vegetable: seed, leaves, flowers and the green beans themselves. This experience is truly worthwhile!

As soon as spring has arrived, a child can sow two or three seeds in a ten-inch (25 cm) diameter pot, filled with potting compost. Place the pot near a sunny window and water regularly so the soil does not become dry.

At the end of a few weeks, the child will notice the seedling and then some leaves. As soon as it is warm enough outside, place the pot in a warm sunny corner of the garden or outside on the balcony, near a fence or a trellis, since this is a climbing plant.

The child will then be able to watch the successive stages of its growth – the flowers, and then the pods themselves will slowly form.

Words can hardly express a child's happiness as he tastes the beans (raw or cooked) which he himself planted.

Let's make homemade bread (activity for a four-year-old and older)

What a thrill to discover in your kitchen that yeast makes dough rise. And what a splendid smell hot bread has as it comes from the oven. What can be more lovely than devouring it warm.

A child who has seen corn fields, knows where flour comes from and has helped to make the bread, has had a unique and unforgettable experience!

Bread-making is simple. However, quite a long time has to be set aside for the dough to rise and for the baking. Morning or early afternoon is the ideal time to start work on the recipe which follows. The baking will coincide with mealtime so that tasting the bread will not spoil a child's appetite.

Whole-Meal Bread

Ingredients
1½ lb. (680 g) whole-wheat flour
8 fl.oz. (250 ml) pint boiling water
2 teaspoons salt
1 tablespoon margarine
5 tablespoons powdered skimmed milk
4 tablespoons honey
6 fl.oz. (250 ml) cold water
1 envelope of yeast sprinkled over 3 fl.oz. (60 ml) lukewarm water
and left for about 10 minutes

Preparation (the mother should carry out the first six steps)
1. Place honey, margarine and salt in a large bowl.
2. Pour in boiling water and mix well.
3. Add cold water and mix until preparation is lukewarm.
4. Add the soaked yeast and mix in half the flour gradually. Mix until smooth.
5. Add powdered milk and beat for two minutes.
6. Add remaining flour and mix well.
7. Knead dough. Show the child how to do this and let him try for a few minutes.
8. When the dough has been well kneaded, brush a little vegetable oil over the top of the dough, cover with a damp cloth, and let the dough rise until it has doubled in volume.
9. Once the dough has doubled, show the child the change; let him punch the dough in the centre and watch it sink down.
10. Knead dough again with help of the child, shape into two small loaves. Place in well-greased bread tins, cover and leave to rise until double in volume. Alternatively: divide the dough into small pieces and let the child mould his own little loaves. Cover with a damp cloth and leave to rise until double in volume in a warm place, while explaining to the child what yeast is and how it makes the dough rise.
11. When the dough has doubled in bulk, cook in a 350°F (180°C) oven until the loaves are golden and crusty (45 to 60 minutes).

Recipe Index

232

233

GENERAL INDEX

Infections
  resistance to *43*
Ingurgitation reflex
  (swallowing) *97*
Iron
  absorption *110*
  electrolytic *110*
  infant supplement *94-5*
  modified milk *94-5*
  mother's milk
  40, 93-4
  nursing mother's supplement
  77-8, 79
  prenatal diet *31-2*
  prenatal supplement *31-4*
  reduced *110*
  role, source, needs *144*
  supplement for infant *93-4*

Lactose
  modified milk *83*
  mother's milk *40, 42,*
La Leche
  League international *49*

Magnesium
  cow's milk *83*
  modified milk *83*
Malnutrition *32, 63*
Manual expression of breast-
  milk *58, 59*
Mastitis *58*
Meals
  atmosphere *21, 152, 165-66*
  participation in *166*
  physical comfort *166*
  schedule after 9 months
  148-50
  timetable *165-66*
  whims *22, 149, 213-14*
Meat
  nursing mother's diet *65*
  poultry *65, 104-5*
  practical guide to
    introduction of *105*
  processed *107*
  proteins *105*
  substitutes *105*
Menus

prenatal *32-3*
Microwave *118-19*
Milk and milk products
  64-5, 164
Modified milks
  comparison with cow's milk
  82-3
  composition *82*
  cost *47-8, 84*
  direction for use *84*
  time of introduction *84, 87*
  nutritive value *82*
  vegetable oils *82*
Mother's milk
  advantages for the baby
  37-39
  anti-diuretic action *42*
  development of brain
  29, 38, 40
  freezing *56-60*
  insufficient milk *58-9*
  mother undernourished *53-4*
  nutritional data *42-3*
  nutritional value *39-41*
  of different mammals *37-8*
  PCBs in *52-3*
  quality and quantity *39-41*

National Childbirth Trust *49, 50*
Neurological development *40*
Niacin
  role, source, needs *138*
Nipple discomfort *58*
Nursing mother's diet
  carnivorous *72-8*
  chocolate *69*
  eggs *65*
  fats *67-8*
  fruits *66-7*
  liquids *68*
  milk produts *64-5*
  meat, poultry, fish *65*
  menus *72-6*
  menus, nutritional value of
  77-9
  pastries and sweets *68*
  problem foods and fluids
  69-70
  supplements *70-1*
  vegetables *67*
  vegetarian *72-9*

236

Other gift books from Exley Publications

What is a Baby? £3.95. (hardback) Parents and grandparents describe the fun and traumas of bringing up baby. A hilarious and beautiful book for any young mother, stunningly illustrated with beautiful photographs.

The Cook's Lifeline, £4.95 (paperback), £9.95 (hardback). Everything the cook needs for the kitchen and where to get it by post. Food, kitchenware, electrical goods, tiling, floors, lighting, storage jars and so forth. A must for the house-proud or the keen cook.

Sharing Nature With Children, £3.50. This book contains over forty games which children can play in the country, in city parks and in their own gardens. The games are fun, but they also bring a real understanding of nature, camouflage, the roles of hunter and hunted, and the natural balance of living things.

Help! I've got a teenager! £6.95 (hardback) A very helpful book for parents tearing their hair out because of their teenagers. The authors are psychologists and joint parents. They offer step-by-step advice on such problems as what to do if your teenager won't clean his or her room, is failing at school or is sexually promiscuous.

Free Stuff for Kids, £4.50. This book will bring a lot of fun to children aged six to thirteen. There are so many things to write for from the Post Office, Nestlé, PG Tips, Kodak, Longleat, Stanley Gibbons and dozens upon dozens of other firms. And they're all either free or up to £1. The book is educational too – it teaches children to write letters and gets them involved in creative hobbies. A very special present, full of potential activity.

Is There Life After Housework? £5.95 (hardback). A revolutionary book which sets out to show how you can save up to 75% of the time you now spend on cleaning. It is written by a man who heads one of the largest cleaning firms in the world. Humorous illustrations throughout. It's a natural gift to the hardpressed and downtrodden!

Grandmas & Grandpas £3.95. (hardback). Children are close to grandparents and this book, written entirely by children, reflects that warmth. 'A Grandma is old on the outside and young on the inside.' An endearing book for grandparents.

Love, a celebration, £4.95. (hardback). Writers and poets old and new have captured the feeling of being in love in this very personal collection. Some of the best love messages of all ages are sensitively illustrated with fine photograms and grey screened photographs. And to enhance the collection the book is bound in a rich wine-red suedel cloth and finished with gold tooling, gift wrapped and sealed with wax. This is our best-selling book – it makes an ideal love-gift.

Marriage, a keepsake, £4.95. (hardback) In the same series as *Love, a celebration*, but with a dove-grey suedel cover. This collection of poems and prose celebrates marriage with some of the finest love messages between husbands and wives. A gift for all ages – from those about to be married to those who have known fifty good years and more together. Giftwrapped with sealing wax.

For Mother, a gift of love. £4.95. (hardback). Also in the same series, this collection of tributes to mothers is bound in pale blue seudel. Rudyard Kipling, Noël Coward, T.B. Macaulay, Victor Hugo, Norman Mailer, C. Day Lewis and Alfred Lord Tennyson are among the contributors. Giftwrapped with sealing wax.

Old is . . .great! £3.25. (hardback). A wicked book of cartoons which pokes fun at youth and revels in the first grey hairs of middle age. 'Extremely funny' (Daily Telegraph).

Free colour catalogue available on request. Books may be ordered through your bookshop, or by post from Exley Publications, Dept FYC1, 16 Chalk Hill, Watford, Herts, United Kingdom WD1 4BN. Please add 50p per book for postage and packing.

Exley Publications reserves the right to show new retail prices on books, which may differ from those previously advertised.